Close to the Edge

CLOSE TO THE EDGE

Moving Beyond Your Comfort Zone

Maurice Vitty
Foreword Andy Economides

XULON PRESS ELITE

Xulon Press
2301 Lucien Way #415
Maitland, FL 32751
407.339.4217
www.xulonpress.com

© 2020 by Maurice Vitty
Formerly Great Exploits or Trivial Pursuit
Copyright © Maurice Vitty 1987, 2020
Foreword © Andy Economides, 2020

All rights reserved solely by the author. The author guarantees all contents are original and do not infringe upon the legal rights of any other person or work. No part of this book may be reproduced in any form without the permission of the author. The views expressed in this book are not necessarily those of the publisher.

The moral right of Maurice Vitty to be identified as the Author of this work has been asserted by him in accordance with the Copyright, Designs, and Patents Act 1988

Unless otherwise indicated, Scripture quotations taken from (Version(s) used)

Typeset by Michelle Cline
Printed and bound in, by

Paperback ISBN-13: 978-1-6312-9834-9
Ebook ISBN-13: 978-1-6312-9835-6

To Hilary,
Sarah, Matt, Abigail, and Jacob

And in memory of three of my great heroes of the faith;
Doreen Snelling (née Cadney), Terrance Roche,
and Margaret Earp

Foreword

MAURICE HAS THE SPIRIT OF JESUS LIVING IN him, and that is partly why I have always liked him. Maurice says in his book that we need to discern between the caution that comes from wisdom and the fear that comes from unbelief. He writes to help us overcome our fear. He writes: "Caleb was not full of himself at all; he was full of the Holy Spirit and of faith! 'We have not received a spirit of fear.'"

Maurice points out that if we follow Jesus fully, we may get into trouble with the world, and even the church. Are we ready for that? Maurice reminds us that we may be misunderstood, but that is part of the price we pay for making our lives count for Christ and His Kingdom. However, even when Jesus was understood He was still rejected. Jesus spoke the truth, He is the truth, and lived a true life. Jesus let people feel the weight of who He was and let them deal with it. Maurice reminds us that this truth is the truth that sets us free.

All through his life the Lord has protected Maurice from danger and disaster, and we can all learn from his life and works. Truly, the safest place for all of us is to be in the center of God's will.

Revd. Andy Economides
Evangelist and Founding Director, Soteria Trust

Reflections from Roger Forster; International Speaker, Author, Church Planter, and Co-Founder of March For Jesus

THIS BOOK IS A REAL PAGE-TURNER! IT WILL challenge you, and cause you to evaluate afresh the level of your faith in Jesus and in His authority and power. Jesus Himself commented on people's faith or lack of it, as when He described His own disciples as "you of little faith" when they panicked in the storm (Matthew 8:26). Then, there was a Roman centurion (Matthew 8:10-12) who had not been brought up with the scriptures of Judaism, but who came to Jesus and addressed Him as Lord. He pleaded with Him to heal his servant who was desperately ill. When Jesus said He would come to the house and heal the man, the centurion showed the depth of his understanding of the authority of Jesus by responding that Jesus did not need to come–He only needed to speak the word and the servant would be healed. When Jesus heard the spiritual insight of the centurion, He marveled and said He had not found such great faith, even in Israel. Of course the servant was healed according to the faith of that Roman centurion! He was a person of "great faith" and so were the apostles once they had conquered their human weakness and learned from Jesus.

The Lord is still looking for people who will grow in faith, and Maurice has written *Close to the Edge* with this in mind. He shows us how to transform our "little faith" into faith that will lay hold of the purposes in God's heart for this world, and bring in His kingdom. *Close to the Edge* is full of stories of men and women of faith who have stepped out boldly for God, including the author's own adventures, many of which we in Ichthus Christian Fellowship, have followed in prayer and encouragement. His use of pictures, parables, proverbs and wise words, and theology from many centuries, makes it an easy and enjoyable read, while drawing out our souls to seek God and walk with Him.

You will discover in these pages that the author was a ship's captain, and he uses the biblical stories about people of faith to navigate us out of the shallows and into the ocean depths of fulness of life. So we will arrive at last at our heavenly haven. Peter, the apostle, puts it in his epistle that we will have "an abundant entry into the everlasting kingdom of our Lord and Saviour Jesus Christ", along with all those who have lived for the Kingdom of God in this world.

Thank you Maurice. "Finishing our course with joy" is the challenge of the message of this book. So may the Holy Spirit fill us with faith and power to fulfil the purposes of God for our earthly lives!

Roger T Forster
London, England
Founder and Leader of Ichthus Christian Fellowship

Acknowledgments

I AM DEEPLY INDEBTED TO THE MANY PEOPLE who have helped me put this book together. Special thanks to my wife, Hilary; also to Adam Charon, Bob Chambers, Nancy Burkhart and Pastor Don Stolhammer. I am grateful too for the facilities made available to me by Oak Hills Bible College in Minnesota. Finally, special thanks to Pastor William Dale Peterson and Ron Spreng (for the gift of the book *Explore the Book* by J. Sidlow Baxter). I would like to thank the members of St. Mildred's Church, London SE12, England, for their commitment to me and belief in my ministry; also the members of the CCP team and the Seacare project, including all the prayer partners, for their loyal and faithful support. I am also grateful to Jenny Page and Joe Laycock for their assistance in the pre-publishing stages of this revised edition, and to Ichthus Christian Fellowship, London. Thank you.

Author's note: Some of the above who helped me do not necessarily agree with every theological point in this book.

Contents

Foreword vii
Reflections from Roger Forster ix
Acknowledgments xi
About This Book xvii

Chapter 1 The Dynamics of Faith (Hebrews 11:1–3) 1

    This Strange Thing Called Faith   4
    How to Increase Our Faith   5
    Lay the Foundation   6
    Talk With the Architect   8

Chapter 2 Faith At the Dawn of History (Hebrews 11:4–7) 11

    The More Excellent Sacrifice   11
    Choose Life   14
    Noah and the Ship Project   16
    Is Jesus in the Boat?   17

Chapter 3 Go With God (Hebrews 11:8) 21

    But Where Are We Going?   21
    The "Who" of Faith   24

**Chapter 4 Battleship to Glory, Or Caribbean Cruise?
(Hebrews 11:9, 10, 13, 14, 16)** 29
   Past Or Present? 30
   God's House Or Ours? 32
   Vision Or Division? 33

Chapter 5 No Turning Back (Hebrews 11:15) 37
   Only a Fool Would Go Back to Egypt 38
   How to Look Down on Giants 39
   The Man or Woman God Uses 40

Chapter 6 Me and My Boy (Hebrews 11:11, 12, 17–19) 45
   I'll Never Forget That Day 46

**Chapter 7 You Call This a Christian Family?
(Hebrews 11:20–22)** 51
   Love Finds a Way 52
   The Power of Forgiveness 57
   Early Retirement? No Thanks! 59

Chapter 8 The Faith of the Leader (Hebrews 11:23–29) 63
   More Than We Ask Or Think 63
   A Wise Choice 64
   The Blood of the Lamb 66
   Faith for Every Emergency 68

Chapter 9 Where the Action Is (Hebrews 11:30–34) 71
   Joshua and the Victory of Faith 74
   In Jericho's Red Light Area 76
   Are You Standing in the Jordan? 77
   Joshua and the Failure of Presumption 79
   And What More Shall I Say? 81

CONTENTS

Chapter 10 Raising the Dead (Hebrews 11:35a) 89
    The Theology   90
    A Word of Warning   94
    The Purpose of Signs and Wonders   95
    Resurrection: The Ultimate Miracle   99
    God In a Box   101

Chapter 11 Faith In the Dark (Hebrews 11:35b–40)   103
    When Things Go Wrong   104
    When the "Props" are Taken Away   104
    When Opposition and Persecution Come   106
    When the Thorn Just Won't Come Out   108
    When Failure and Discouragement Come   111
    When Death Comes   113

Chapter 12 The Challenge of the Impossible (Hebrews 12:1–2)   117
    Run With God   123
    Get Up and Grow   124

Postscript   *127*

Notes   *129*

About This Book

JAMES SAID THAT FAITH WITHOUT WORKS IS dead (James 2:26). This book is about action as much as it is about faith. There are many excellent books explaining the doctrine of faith; this book focuses in on the action-filled life that should result from such understanding.

I have written this book for all who want to increase their faith. I hope it will be particularly helpful to those who are about to embark on an ambitious project, an adventure of faith, or those who are just not willing to sit back and fritter their lives away.

I have chosen Daniel 11:32b and Hebrews 11 as my texts, and have sought to treat these Scriptures seriously. I hope that you will find much spiritual food in the pages of this book. I have not drawn back from tackling some of the more difficult principles in Hebrews 11, and have attempted to show how up to date and relevant they are for all of us.

In writing a book on one particular theme there is always the danger of presenting an unbalanced view. For example, we can do all these great exploits and exercise tremendous faith, but "if we have not love. . ." (1 Corinthians 13). Please bear this in mind as you read on.

Also in the interests of balance, I take for granted that you are earnestly seeking God's will for your life. I refer to this on more than one occasion in the pages of this book because it is so easy to cross the line from faith to presumption. The principles of faith outlined in this book work; but they should be applied to what God wants to do through you, not what you've decided you're going to do for Him. I have also tried to show you how to discern the difference.

I have sought to be creative in my writing, so you will come across fictionalized accounts, like the story of Abraham and Isaac being told from Abraham's viewpoint, for example. I hope this gives insight and makes the book more enjoyable.

Finally, I want to make it clear that God does put people in what seem (compared to some of the "heroes" of the faith) like unimportant or mediocre positions. This book is not meant to make such people feel inadequate. The most important position anyone can be in is at the center of God's will. Shining for Jesus in a secular situation can be the hardest calling of all.

The principles of faith you will learn in this book will help you too in accomplishing the great exploit of being salt in your community. In fact, this is what the book of Daniel is all about—living out the faith in a pagan culture. Some translations of Daniel 11:32 ("Those who do wickedly against the covenant he shall corrupt with flattery; but the people who know their God shall be strong, and carry out great exploits.") use the term "resist" instead of "carry out great exploits," because the context refers to standing up to fierce satanic onslaught. What could be more relevant than that today?

So whatever your situation—pioneer missionary, office worker, evangelist, wife and mother, shop-floor worker or pastor—the message of this book is for you. I hope you will draw strength and encouragement from it and renew your vision of our great God, because it is only "the people who know their God" who will "be strong, and carry out great exploits."

Maurice Vitty, London, England, 2020

Chapter 1
The Dynamics of Faith

Now faith is the substance of things hoped for, the evidence of things not seen. For by it the elders obtained a good testimony.

By faith we understand that the worlds were framed by the word of God, so that the things which are seen were not made of things which are visible.

Hebrews 11:1–3

The blade of the flick knife looked very scary. I didn't doubt that its owner would use it. I had just learned what not to say when witnessing late at night to a drunken, drugged-up member of a motorcycle gang! Remember this in case you're ever in that situation—don't ever say that you're not afraid to die because you know you're going to heaven. If you do, you may well meet with this response: "So, you're not afraid to die, huh? Well, we'll see about that!" And then you'll find yourself looking down the blade of a lethal weapon, asking the Lord if, now that you've learned this lesson, He might give you another chance with someone else!

Now, I'm a coward, so what happened next surprised me more than anyone. Somehow, the Lord gave me His peace. I knew that I was going about my Father's business, and that He was going to take care of me, so I simply smiled at my would-be assailant. At this, a look of sheer terror came across his face, and the next thing I knew, he and his friend were tearing down the road as fast as their legs would carry them.

Jackie Pullinger was a young girl, brought up in a nice, respectable part of Britain, with a fine career in music ahead of her. However, God had other plans. He led her to Hong Kong, where she pioneered a work of God's Spirit among drug addicts, prostitutes and Triad gangsters. Hardened criminals turned to Christ in the dark alleys of Kowloon's infamous Walled City. When asked if she ever became frightened of the Triads, she replied, "No, when they see me coming down the street, it is they who are frightened."[1]

When King Asa had to go into battle against an army twice the size of his own, he cried out to the Lord and said, "Lord, it is nothing for You to help . . ." (2 Chronicles 14:11a). I wonder if today we have fully understood that whatever situation we face, it is nothing for God to help?

It's not that our testimony finds its power in the fact that God can look after us. No, the real strength of our message is that nothing can separate us from the love of Christ, neither death nor life (Romans 8:38–39); more on this in Chapter 11. Whatever happens, we are on the winning side. As Jesus said to Pilate before He was crucified, "You could have no power at all against Me unless it had been given you from above" (John 19:11a). Have we really understood the implications of that statement for us today?

Consider these words of Jesus:

> Most assuredly, I say to you, he who believes in Me, the works that I do he will do also; and greater works than these he will do, because I go to My Father. And whatever you ask in My name, that I will do, that the Father may be glorified in the

Son. If you ask anything in my name, I will do it.
(John 14:12–14)

Everything is possible for him who believes.
(Mark 9:23)

Would you pause for a moment and consider whether or not you really believe those words of Jesus? If your answer is no, then ask Him to increase your faith; if yes, then you must be as excited as I am at what God has promised to do through ordinary people like you and me, if only we believe.

The Holy Spirit once spoke to Rees Howells saying, "It is the Father's will to restore your uncle." It seemed "too good to be true, and too great to believe." Mr. Howells' uncle had been an invalid for thirty years and totally unable to walk. The Holy Spirit then confirmed this directly to the uncle by telling him that he would be healed in exactly four and a half months, on May 15. When they looked this date up on the calendar, they discovered it was Pentecost Sunday. The Holy Spirit confirmed that the uncle would indeed be healed in memory of Pentecost, and that it would be at five o'clock in the morning.

Many of the local people pitied the uncle, thinking that he had allowed himself to be led astray. His condition, far from improving, actually got worse. Despite the scoffing, Mr. Howells' Uncle Dick confidently declared that he would be healed at 5 A.M. on Whit Sunday and would walk the three miles to church and back.

On the night before Whit Sunday, Uncle Dick was as bad as ever. He had to get out of bed at 1 A.M. because of the discomfort. Eventually, at 2 A.M., he fell into a deep sleep. "The next thing he heard was the clock striking five, and he found himself completely restored." The rest of the family was struck with awe as they realized that God Himself had healed him that very hour. He walked unaided to church and never had another day's illness in his life.[2]

Why do we not see this kind of faith in the church today? Perhaps we've become too busy discussing doctrine, and have forgotten one all-important fact: that the God of all the universe and

His Son, the Savior of the world, have found somewhere to live—inside of you and me (John 14:23)! The fullness of God dwells within our hearts. No wonder our enemies scatter!

This Strange Thing Called Faith

> Now faith is the substance of things hoped for, the evidence of things not seen. For by it the elders obtained a good testimony. (Hebrews 11:1–2)

God gave Hebrews 11:1 to Rees Howells and his uncle as they trusted Him for four and a half months for "the substance of things hoped for and the evidence of things not seen."

Have you ever considered faith as a substance? The word "substance" implies something tangible, something that we can lay hold of. The word "evidence" brings to mind something tangible too—proof. Yet we are talking of that which is "hoped for," that which is "not seen." The healing of a relative, the conversion of a friend, the revival of a nation!

When Dr. John Geddie went to Aneityum, Vanuatu in 1848, he could not see any work of God going on. Yet, with the eyes of faith he could see the work that God wanted to do, and so he offered himself to "stand in the gap" (Ezekiel 22:30). He labored there for twenty-four years. On a tablet erected in his memory are inscribed these words:

> When he landed, in 1848, there were no Christians.
> When he left, in 1872, there were no heathen.[3]

Yes, by faith the elders obtained a good testimony. The church left behind in Aneityum was the substance of that which Geddie hoped for, and the evidence of the unseen work of God's Holy Spirit.

Loren Cunningham once had a vision, a literal picture in his mind, of waves and waves of young people moving out.[4] This vision materialized into a worldwide missionary endeavor of young people known today as Youth With A Mission.

The young Billy Graham, in 1938, surrendered his life to the will of God, which he sensed was the call to preach the gospel. Twenty-five years later he recalled, "In the most unusual way I used to have the strangest glimpses of these great crowds I now preach to."[5] Yes, the substance of things hoped for, the evidence of things not seen. And what elder on the face of the whole earth obtained a better testimony than Dr. Billy Graham?

Let's recap:

- The man or woman of faith is able to see what God wants to do.
- The man or woman of faith is willing to "stand in the gap."
- The man or woman of faith acts as a channel for the Spirit of God to bring into physical being that which is invisible.

How to Increase Our Faith

The spiritual gift of faith mentioned in 1 Corinthians 12:9 is given by God to particular members of the Body of Christ for specific situations. Whether we have this gift or not does not release us from the need to be a people who live by faith.

Before we seek to grow in this area though, we should first do some honest heart-searching. We should begin by asking ourselves the following questions:

1. Why do I want to increase my faith? What are my motives?
2. What will I do with this increase in faith when I get it?
3. Have I counted the cost of what this may involve for my future?
4. Am I sincerely seeking to glorify God?

Do not be unduly concerned if you cannot sort out all of your motives. These questions are not designed to stop us from going forward, merely to stop us from *rushing* forward. Let us work through these questions, then press on.

Having determined why we want to increase our faith, and what we are going to do with it once we have it, we now come to the all-important question. How? At this point we need to divert our attention away from the word "faith," to the word "God"—who is, after all, the object of our faith. I believe that the key to unlocking the storehouse of faith and adventure is found not only in a study of faith but also in a study of God. That is why I have chosen to look at Daniel 11:32 alongside the famous faith chapter, Hebrews 11. Daniel, in one sentence, has shown us what the life of faith is all about.

> The people who *know their God* shall be strong, and carry out great exploits (italics mine).

Knowing God is the key—not knowing *about* Him! We are not talking about a transfer of knowledge about God from the Bible to our memory; we are talking about an intimate personal relationship with Him through Jesus Christ.

You see, faith is nothing more than believing in someone whom you trust, and you never know if you can trust someone until you get to know them.

A minister friend of mine discovered that his elder sister had been diagnosed as having terminal cancer. He made a long-distance telephone call to console her. However, she didn't need as much consolation as might have been expected. He told me that he would never forget what she said to him: "I've trusted God for sixty years. I'm not about to stop now." A lady of faith? Certainly, but more importantly, a lady who knew the One she had put her trust in. She was healed of cancer and lived for many more years, continuing to witness for the Lord. The people who know their God shall be strong!

LAY THE FOUNDATION

There are those around today who teach that faith in faith is all we need. As long as we have faith in something, that is all that really matters. This is nonsense. If our faith is not in One who is worthy of it, One who is almighty, all-powerful, who has our best interests at heart, and who can "deliver the goods," then we will have built our lives on a shaky foundation.

I once heard the story of some rebels involved in the Congo war. The Congolese government had brought in highly trained mercenaries to quell the rebel uprising, which drove the rebels further and further back into the jungle. Finally they went to a village witch doctor. He mixed up a white potion which he assured them would give them victory. So the rebels, having smeared the white liquid all over their bodies, went boldly out to meet the mercenaries. Of course, they were slaughtered. They had faith, but the focus of their faith was all wrong.

Only God is worthy of our trust. The world today is full of false prophets offering false hope. In comparison, Paul tells the Romans that we Christians have a hope that does not disappoint (Romans 5:5a).

The American people were badly shaken by the Watergate scandal. They felt that they had a right to expect the man they had elected to the position of President to be trustworthy. When he failed them, they were bewildered.

I think we are right to expect our leaders to be trustworthy. However, it is very easy for those without God, and sometimes even for those with God, to make these leaders into idols and to almost worship them. No human being can ever fill that God-created vacuum in our hearts. Christ is the only one worthy of such trust, the only one who can be completely relied on. As the hymn writer said.

> On Christ the solid rock I stand;
> All other ground is sinking sand.[6]

Talk With the Architect

> By faith we understand that the worlds were framed by the word of God, so that things which are seen were not made of things which are visible. (Hebrews 11:3)

The natural man, that is, the nonbeliever, has tried to come up with his own theories to explain the creation of the universe. We will not get into debating that whole issue here; suffice to say that, in my opinion, these theories require much more faith than the creationist view. The Christian, however, trusts the simple statement in Genesis 1:1: "In the beginning God created the heavens and the earth." He trusts this statement because he knows that the One who said it can be trusted.

In 1973, Colonel Jack Lousma spent nearly sixty days in space aboard Skylab 2, circling the earth. He says, "As we learn more about the universe, we come to know its Creator more fully and to appreciate Him in a greater way. The whole universe operates in perfect harmony and order, like a finely tuned watch. Only Almighty God could put it together and keep it running so perfectly."[7]

Colonel Lousma likes to study the passages in God's Word that relate to the universe. One of his favorite passages is Psalm 19:1–6:

> The heavens are telling the glory of God; they are a marvelous display of His craftsmanship. Day and night they keep on telling about God. Without a sound or word, silent in the skies, their message reaches out to all the world. The sun lives in the heavens where God placed it and moves out across the skies as radiant as a bridegroom going to his wedding, or as joyous as an athlete looking forward to a race. The sun crosses the heavens from end to end, and nothing can hide from its heat. (TLB)

Whatever you may think about the Crystal Cathedral in California, you may be interested to know that its founders, Robert H. Schuller and his wife Arvella, worked closely with the architect for eighteen years.[8] How much more should we be working with the Architect of the universe and the whole human race? Our task is to build faith into our lives, and we won't get far without a good working relationship with the Master Designer Himself.

It's very easy for prayer to become nothing more than a religious duty or, at best, the submitting of a list of requests. We need to recapture the vision for times of sweet communion with the Savior. Consider what the Lord once said to Solomon:

> If My people who are called by My name will humble themselves, and pray and seek my face . . .
> (2 Chronicles 7:14)

Show me those who are seeking His face, and I will show you great exploits. Show me a great work of the Spirit of God, and I will show you somebody down on his knees. Show me a revival, and I will show you a whole fellowship of believers down on their knees.

I shall always be grateful for the opportunity I had to serve with Operation Mobilization. I don't remember a single prayer meeting during the time I was with them that lasted less than five hours—usually they were nearer six or seven. No wonder God has mightily blessed that work.

Don't treat God like a vending machine, cold and impersonal, someone you just stop and spend a few moments with when you need something. Seek His face, worship and adore Him, tell Him that you love Him and you want to get to know Him. He is waiting to work with you. Talk to Him.

Listen to Him. A relationship has to be two-way for it to be a relationship at all. There are many ways to listen to God: He speaks through His Word, He speaks through other Christians, He speaks through sermons and He speaks through songs and psalms. He also speaks directly into our hearts through the still, small voice of the Holy Spirit.

There are some today who will have nothing to do with anything as subjective as still, small voices. However, can we really enter into a personal relationship with God without such subjectivity? No, it is impossible. Provided this subjectivity is submitted to sound biblical principles, we have nothing to fear.

In his book *Is That Really You, God?*, Loren Cunningham tells of how he used to approach a time of prayer with a view to listening to what God was saying through the promptings of the Holy Spirit. This intrigued me, so we tried it in our mission. Let me tell you, it works. For example, Sue Witham, our administrator, received the word "Scunthorpe." Of course, it meant nothing to her at all. She did not know that this was my hometown, in North Lincolnshire, England. Later, she remembered a dynamic Christian lady who lived in Scunthorpe and decided to renew contact with her. This led to the lady, Rene Hargreaves, joining our mission. I have no doubt at all that this was the work of the Holy Spirit.

In Gordon MacDonald's book *Ordering Your Private World* he tells us how, for twenty years, he has kept a journal to record God's whispers. He says, "With pencil in hand ready to write, I found that there was an expectancy, a readiness to hear anything that God might whisper through my reading and reflection."[9]

Take time to cultivate that relationship with the Living God. He is our power source. Without Him, we can do nothing. With Him, all things are possible. As we proceed through the pages of this book, we will learn many principles of faith, and how to turn that faith into action. But above all, I pray that we will renew our vision of our great God. Then, like the prophet Jeremiah, we too will be able to say:

> Ah, Lord God! Behold, You have made the heavens and the earth by Your great power and outstretched arm. There is nothing too hard for You. (Jeremiah 32:17)

Chapter 2
Faith At the Dawn of History

The More Excellent Sacrifice

> By faith Abel offered to God a more excellent sacrifice than Cain, through which he obtained witness that he was righteous, God testifying of his gifts; and through it he being dead still speaks. (Hebrews 11:4)

Hudson Taylor once said, "God's work, done God's way, will not lack God's supply."[1] I have literally staked my life on that statement. A foolish thing to do, perhaps, when it is not Holy Scripture? No, not at all, for it is in fact an example of Scripture. Take Matthew 6:33, "But seek first the kingdom of God and His righteousness, and all these things shall be added to you." Hudson Taylor was right on target! He was a man who knew his God.

When we decided at the beginning of our ministry on a policy of making our needs known to God alone, I never once anticipated all the trouble it would lead to. There has hardly been a day when we haven't felt pressure to compromise our position. It was as if we had broken some kind of unwritten law. Perhaps we were no longer playing by the rules; but who established those rules? Certainly not God.

Does God give His people a blank check? I believe the answer to that question is—yes! Provided they are:

1. doing His work; that is, the specific work He wants them to do, and
2. doing it His way; that is, in a way that glorifies Him.

I can offer no other explanation for the provision I have seen when, while traveling around the world with no money, I have trusted Him each step of the way. Nor can I explain why the only times the resources have not been provided have been when I've stepped out of His will, whether in terms of direction or methods. What a safeguard this policy is if we are seriously concerned about His glory. I don't disagree with fundraising, if that's what God has called you to do. We just had to be obedient to the way He led us.

My family and I had just spent nine months in America, studying, preaching and traveling around spreading the vision for Seacare (our rescue ship project). We decided not to take any support from our mission but to look to God alone. Not once did we go without anything. The Lord would provide enough finance for a few weeks, then, at the exact moment that ran out, He would provide the next installment. One gift we received was for over one thousand pounds. He alone knew our needs and He alone met them.

I have never believed that asking for money is wrong, but what I would question is, is it necessary? Of course, there are organizations that exist with the prime goal of raising money for the Lord's work. They are a different matter, and I wouldn't dispute what they are doing for one moment. Some organizations, though, have deceived themselves into thinking that what they are doing is so important that the end justifies the means. It is very sad to see Christian organizations following the world's example as regards raising funds. Oh, how this must grieve our God; and it's unnecessary if we are committed to doing His work in His way.

Now I hear you say, "What's all this got to do with Cain and Abel?" I believe it has everything to do with them, for both of these men offered a sacrifice to God, but only one of their sacrifices was accepted. There are many Christian works going on in the world today, but are they all accepted? Before we can claim God's promises through faith, we have to meet the conditions. God's work has to be done in God's way.

The difference between Cain and Abel was the difference between the life in the flesh and the life in the Spirit; and that's all the difference in the world.

Frank Sinatra made the song "My Way" an enormous success, but that one lyric, "I did it my way," explains why many ministries end in failure. We will insist on doing it our way, and that just is not an acceptable sacrifice to bring before our God.

Archbishop William Temple once said:

> For there is only one sin and it is characteristic of the whole world. It is the self-will that prefers my way to God's—which puts me in the center where only God is in place. It pervades the universe. It accounts for the cruelty of the jungle, where each animal follows its own appetite, unchecked and unable to heed any general good. It becomes conscious, and thereby tenfold more virulent in man—a veritable fall indeed.[2]

Cain was a carnal man. He was probably arrogant and proud, and lived the life of the flesh to the full. In Genesis 4:7 we are told that Cain had not mastered sin in his life.

In comparison, Abel had a more realistic view of himself, recognizing that he was just a sinner saved by grace. Even though the Levitical laws concerning the blood and fat of animals had not yet been instituted (Leviticus 3:16), it didn't stop him from coming before his God with "the firstlings of his flock and of their fat" as a sin offering. I feel sure that Cain and Abel must be very similar to the Pharisee and the tax collector in Luke 18:10–14. Cain probably thanked God that he wasn't like Abel. Abel, on the other hand, humble and contrite, just brought his sin offering.

If we are still living the life of the flesh, it will show itself in the way we run our churches and Christian organizations; the way we struggle for position, the way we become so easily threatened, the way we compete with each other and, of course, the way we go about raising money.

Psalm 51:17 shows us what an acceptable sacrifice is:

> The sacrifices of God are a broken spirit,
> A broken and a contrite heart—
> These, O God, You will not despise.

Let's recap: The man or woman who has let God break him or her of pride is a man or woman who:

- does not need to compete
- is not easily threatened
- is not driven by ambition, but is led by the Holy Spirit
- seeks to build God's kingdom, not his or her own empire
- is not a lone ranger (even he had Tonto!), but functions as part of the body
- is well able to trust everything to the God he or she knows so well

Obedience does not come cheap; it cost Abel his life. However, the cost of disobedience is not cheap either, for Cain became a fugitive and vagabond on the earth. For the rest of his life he was away from the presence of the Lord. And where are Cain and Abel now? Our Hebrews text tells us that Abel, even though he is dead, still speaks (Hebrews 11:4). It has nothing, nothing at all to say about Cain.

Choose Life

> By faith Enoch was taken away so that he did not see death, "and was not found, because God had

taken him;" for before he was taken he had this testimony, that he pleased God. (Hebrews 11:5)

Andrew Murray once said, "God has no more precious gift to a church or an age than a man who lives as an embodiment of His will, and inspires those around him with the faith of what grace can do."[3] Such a man was Enoch.

At the age of sixty-five, Enoch begat Methuselah. This makes him Noah's great-grandfather; Lamech, Noah's father, being the son of Methuselah. After Methuselah was born, we are told that Enoch began to walk with God (Genesis 5:22). This he was to do for the next three hundred years before he was literally translated directly to heaven.

How this man, who consistently walked with God, must have inspired those around him! And what a testimony to the grace of God. Enoch was not one to fall back on excuses; he could easily have said, "Well, I'm just a descendant of Adam—I've inherited a sinful nature. You must make allowances for me." But no; Enoch chose to walk with God.

In Deuteronomy 30:19 God says, "I have set before you life and death, blessing and cursing; therefore choose life, that both you and your descendants may live." Enoch did just this; he chose life, and God granted life both to him and to his descendant, Noah, who was later spared when God flooded the world.

We have the same choice before us that Enoch had. Will we:

- choose life and live?
- choose life and inspire others?
- choose life and please God?

When people look at us, are they immediately struck by the testimony of what grace can do? If not, then maybe we've been making the wrong choices.

Noah and the Ship Project

> By faith Noah, being divinely warned of things not yet seen, moved with godly fear, prepared an ark for the saving of his household, by which he condemned the world and became heir of the righteousness which is according to faith. (Hebrews 11:7)

I will never forget the first time that I alone was responsible for the navigation of a ship across an entire ocean. We were sailing from the Gulf of Mexico to Cape Town. Once we had left the Caribbean, we did not see land again for weeks, until our arrival off South Africa. We took sights of the sun during the day and from the stars at night. Daily we plotted our position on the chart, basing our calculations entirely on a method formulated by the French naval officer Marcq St. Hilaire. We had no means of confirming whether our position was correct. On the day we were due to arrive, the captain enquired of me, "Well, Second Mate, when are we going to see land?" Somewhat hesitantly I replied, "We should get a glimpse of something by about noon, sir." From about eleven o'clock onward all I did was observe the horizon. At eleven fifty I had quite a sweat on; but sure enough, just before twelve the spectacular view of Table Mountain peeked up above the horizon! I wasn't even a Christian at that time, but I had received a lesson in faith that I would not forget.

Faith does not need to see something to know that it is there. At night we cannot see the sun but we know that we shall in the morning. Jesus said to doubting Thomas, "Because you have seen Me, you have believed. Blessed are those who have not seen and yet have believed" (John 20:29).

God had warned Noah of a coming flood. It could not be seen, but that didn't matter; God could be believed. That's faith! On the basis of this, Noah embarked on one of the most outrageous projects of all history. He built an ark. What project lies before you? For me, it was not unlike Noah's, involving a ship. For you it might be a missionary venture, a church extension, opening a Christian bookshop, starting a Bible study group or Christian Union, rebuilding a marriage, or starting a local nursery. Whatever your project, the question is, "Are you going to step out in faith and trust Him?"

In the days of Noah, violence filled the earth (Genesis 6:11). God decided that for the sake of future generations He would institute a moral salvage operation. Wickedness would literally be washed away by the waters of the coming flood. "But Noah found grace in the eyes of the Lord" (Genesis 6:8). So Noah and his family would be saved.

Today, violence and wickedness fill the earth, and God's ultimate moral salvage operation draws nearer and nearer. Those who trust in Jesus and find grace in the eyes of the Lord will be saved.

To book a berth on Noah's ship, you had to be part of his family. To book a berth on God's ship, that is, the fellow*ship* of believers, you need to be part of God's family. You can do that by admitting that you've been going your own way too long, and by turning to Jesus Christ. Only those who trust in Him shall be saved. Feel inadequate? That you'll never make it? "But as many as received Him, to them He gave the right to become children of God" (John 1:12).

Is Jesus in the Boat?

Once Jesus got into a boat with His disciples and fell asleep (Luke 8:22–25). The wind brewed up a storm and the disciples were terrified. Jesus slept on. The waves got higher, and water started to pour over the gunwale into the boat itself. Jesus slept like a baby. The boat was tossed to and fro; up it would go, high on the crest of a wave, then thud, down into the trough. The timbers creaked and groaned. Jesus slept on. Alas, the disciples could stand no more. They woke Him up; "Master, Master, we are perishing!" Jesus got up and calmly rebuked the wind and the sea, and all was calm again; except that now the disciples were more afraid of Him than they had been of the sea.

Another time, the disciples were again in a storm at sea (Mark 6:45–52). This time Jesus walked out to them on the water, saying, "Be of good cheer! It is I; do not be afraid." Then, as Jesus stepped into the boat, the storm stopped.

You see, the real question for Noah, and for anyone embarking on a project, is not, "Is this too big?" or "Will this make me a laughing stock?" No, the real question is this: *"Is Jesus in the boat?"* Noah built an ark because God had told him to. God was in the boat. It is a foolish thing to embark upon a great project without the assurance that God has called you to it.

Dr. David Yonggi Cho, now retired, was the pastor of the world's largest church, located in Seoul, South Korea. He tells the story of two young ministers who had a similar burden to build a church, but their project was a disaster.

> Then they both came to me. They cried, "Pastor Cho, why is your God and our God different? You started with $2,500, and now you have completed a five million dollar project. We went out and built things which cost only a total of $80,000. Why wouldn't God answer us?"

Dr. Cho replied:

> I started my church because of Rhema (the spoken word), not just Logos (the written word). God clearly spoke to my heart saying, "Rise up, go out and build a church which will seat ten thousand people." God imparted His faith to my heart, and I went out and a miracle occurred. But you went out just with logos, a general knowledge about God and His faith. God therefore has no responsibility to support you, even though your ministry was for the Lord Jesus Christ.[4]

We are told that Noah, like his great-grandfather before him, "walked with God" (Genesis 6:9). If we are going to know God's specific will and purposes, then we need to be walking closely with Him. Before we dare cast off the ropes and set sail, we must be sure that Jesus is in the boat.

Before sailing, check the following:

- Where did the vision or burden for your project come from?
- Has it been bathed in prayer?
- Does it correspond with God's written Word?
- Has it been submitted to the elders of the church (or similar governing body)?
- Would you go some other way if you had a choice?
- Do you have a deep inner conviction and assurance that it is God's specific will, as far as you can tell?
- Is it the right time?

Only now can you let go, hoist the sails, and run with the wind of the Spirit of God. Yes, go with God. Storms may rage, winds may blow; but all is well with your soul, for Jesus is in your boat.

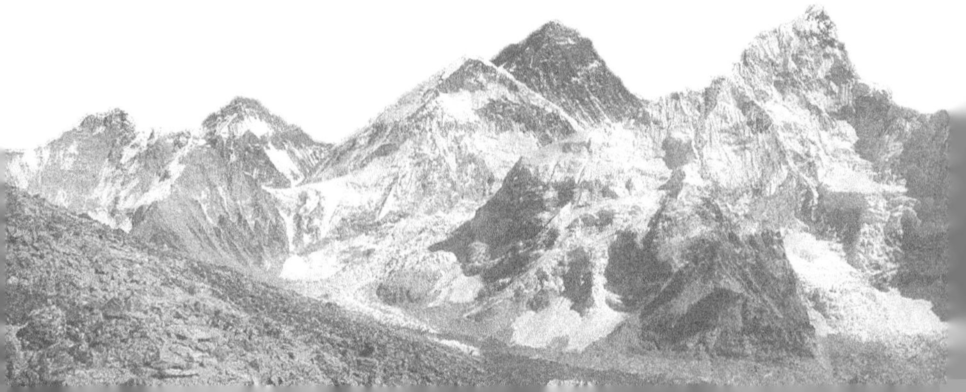

Chapter 3
GO WITH GOD

By faith Abraham obeyed . . . And he went out, not knowing where he was going.

Hebrews 11:8

BUT WHERE ARE WE GOING?

IMAGINE THAT I WAS AT CHURCH ONE SUNDAY morning and felt sure in my heart that God was speaking to me. Our conversation might have gone something like this:

"Maurice, I want you to get out of your seat (no, it wasn't Billy Graham, it was God!), turn around, and walk right out of this place."

"You cannot be serious, Lord, surely not. Where would I go?"

"Outside you will find a car parked with its engine running. It is waiting for you."

"For me? I don't understand."

"The driver works for me."

"But where are we going?"

"Do you really need to know? I will be with you."

"But when will we return?"

"It is not for you to know."

"Uh, we will be returning, won't we?"

"It is not a concern of yours."

"Well, that's okay, but there are a few things to clear up here first: investments, business, that type of thing. It would be irresponsible to leave those things. I've worked my whole life to build up the business. If I leave now—well, frankly, I would have to close down. I would be considered a failure."

"It is written that the seed that fell among thorns is he who hears the word, but the cares of this world and the deceitfulness of riches choke the word and he becomes unfruitful."[1]

"Ah yes, but how do I know you are who you say you are? It is no easy thing to know God's will."

"You know."

"Where will I live?"

"Foxes have holes and the birds of the air have nests, but the Son of Man has nowhere to lay His head."[2]

"But I'm doing the reading at Joe's funeral on Thursday."

"Let the dead bury their own dead."[3]

"Okay, but let me arrange a sending-out service first. I need to say goodbye, don't I?"

"No one having put his hand to the plow, and looking back, is fit for the kingdom of God."[4]

"Now wait a minute, I don't have to take that from anybody. I've been to Bible college, you know. I've taught in Sunday school, and I've preached. I don't know how you can say that someone like me is not fit for the kingdom of God."

"Oh, what did you learn at Bible college?"

"Theology."

"So you know all about me?"

---

[1] Matthew 13:22

[2] Luke 9:58–60

[3] Luke 9:58–60

[4] Luke 9:62

"Yes, you're omnipotent and omniscient. The Greek word for you is Theos—did you know that?"

"I can see you do know *about* me, but do you know me?"

"I thought I had just explained that."

"No, I don't think you did."

"Well, anyway, I got straight As, and I majored in Hermeneutics, which is the art and science of Bible interpretation."

"Very impressive, and really, I'm glad that you took the time out to study, but will you get into that car?"

"Well, it all depends on where it's going. I'm not stupid."

"Why does it depend on where it's going?"

"To help me decide if it's God's will."

"Will you get in?"

"Is it going to the airport? Will I have to travel far away, and eat weird food? The sun burns my skin easily, you know."

"Why do you keep on worrying about where it's going? That's not the important point."

"What is the important point, then?"

"I'll be in the car too."

"I suppose that is kind of comforting, but what will we eat? Where will our support come from? Cars don't run on nothing."

"Do not worry. I am not unaware of this. Seek first My kingdom and My righteousness, and I will work out the other details."

"You make it sound so easy."

"The car is waiting."

"I get travel sick."

"Don't you and your wife have a child?"

"Yes, we have a little girl," I said, thinking to myself, "If He's God, He should know that."

"Well now, tell me, when you and your wife go for a drive in the car, do you explain to your little girl all the details of the journey? Do you tell her where you're going and when you will be back?"

"No, of course not. She's only a child."

"But doesn't she get scared?"

"Why should she? She knows that we will look after her. I'm her father, aren't I? She will be safe with me, and she knows that."

"I see that, yes, I really do, I like that very much. Now will you get in the car?"

"I'll think about it, Lord. I do believe you're trying to show me something here. I'll definitely think about it."

"Well alright, Maurice. You know I'm very patient. I will tell the driver to wait just a little longer. But Maurice . . ."

"Yes?"

"I mean, just a *little* longer."

The "Who" of Faith

You're right, this conversation never did take place; but I hope you will permit my imagination this little indulgence to make a point. How would we respond in a situation like this? Would we be full of excuses or would we, like Abram, simply obey?

Now the Lord had said to Abram:

> Get out of your country,
> From your family
> And from your father's house,
> To a land that I will show you.
> I will make you a great nation;
> I will bless you
> And make your name great;
> And you shall be a blessing.
> I will bless those who bless you,
> And I will curse him who curses you;
> And in you all the families of the earth shall be blessed."
> So Abram departed as the Lord had spoken to him, and Lot went with him. And Abram was seventy-five years old when he departed from Haran. (Genesis 12:1–4)

So, here we have a seventy-five-year-old man. Alright, granted they lived longer in those days, but he was still no spring chicken. And without any arguments or complaints he steps out in faith and total obedience. It was the same, you might recall, when Jesus called the first disciples:

> And Jesus, walking by the Sea of Galilee, saw two brothers, Simon called Peter, and Andrew his brother, casting a net into the sea; for they were fishermen. Then He said to them, "Follow Me, and I will make you fishers of men."
> They immediately left their nets and followed Him. Going on from there, He saw two other brothers, James the son of Zebedee, and John his brother, in the boat with Zebedee their father, mending their nets. He called them, and immediately they left the boat and their father, and followed Him. (Matthew 4:18–22)

We should not merely gloss over these verses as "the time Jesus called the first disciples." There is too much here of vast importance to simply take it for granted.

Notice that we are told in both cases that the disciples immediately left everything and followed this total stranger. Now that is quite an event! You spend your whole life building up a fishing business. It's a family business; dad is involved as well. There's the boat to maintain, the nets to repair. There's the fish to take home to provide food for the families. There's more fish to be taken to market to be sold. You're settled, content, and very happy. All those years of hard work have finally paid off, and now you're sitting pretty! Then suddenly Jesus walks by. He just appears from nowhere with this bright idea of throwing in the business and following Him to fish for men. Who has ever heard of fishing for men?

And the most amazing thing about all of this is—you buy it! You don't ask questions, you just get up and go. Goodbye business, goodbye family, I'm off to fish for men and women with Jesus. Incredible!

What happened to the disciples is exactly the same as what happened to Abraham two thousand years before. The disciples knew beyond any shadow of a doubt that they had heard the voice of God. It all happened so quickly; they weren't at all expecting it. They were merely going about their everyday business when God Himself stepped into their lives in a most amazing way. In an instant they were transformed from humble fishermen to some of the most important men in the history of the world. In Jesus, they saw God.

Philip once asked Jesus to show him the Father (John 14:8). Jesus responded by explaining that whoever saw Him, saw the Father also. Simon, Andrew, James and John knew that they were in the presence of God, and responded accordingly. When we look at God in Jesus, when we consider Him who loved us so much that He died on a cross so that we might live, how can we not be like Abraham and those first disciples? How can we not say, "Yes, Lord," and get up and go?

Isaiah had a vision of God "high and lifted up, and the train of His robe filled the temple" (Isaiah 6:1–8). After this experience, Isaiah felt unclean and had to get right with God. Having done this, he did not hesitate when he heard God saying, "Who will go for us?" His offer was immediate: "Here am I! Send me."

Moses had a similar experience. He came face to face with the power and presence of God in the burning bush. After this he received his commission to go to Egypt.

Are you in touch with God? You may not have a vision or hear a voice, but are you getting through? Is your relationship personal and intimate? Do you expect God to answer your prayers? In Deuteronomy 4:29, God told the children of Israel that wherever He put them, if they would seek Him, they would find Him, providing they sought Him with all their heart and soul. Matthew picks up on this in the New Testament: "... seek, and you will find" (Matthew 7:7). And this brings us back to Hebrews 11:6:

> But without faith it is impossible to please Him, for he who comes to God must believe that

He is, and that He is a rewarder of those who diligently seek Him.

Do you believe this? Then seek Him, believe in Him, put all your trust in Him. He will reward you, for He has promised. He is your trustworthy Father who never fails His children. Do you want to make your Father happy? Without faith it is impossible; but oh, how He delights to see His children trust Him. By faith press on to God.

When we get through to Him, He who is perfect love, all fear will be driven out. Then we will have the faith of Abraham. We will go wherever He calls; we will humbly obey without question. We will say, "I am going with you, Lord, wherever it may be, whatever it may mean, as long as I can be with you." The true servant of Jesus Christ is only interested in being at the center of God's will. He will follow the Master. He does not ask, "Why?" "What?" "How?" "When?" or "Where?" He asks, "Who?" "Are you in it, Lord? Is this you speaking to me? Will you be there?"

This principle has been the rule of many great men and women of God throughout the ages. Moses once prayed to God, "If Your Presence does not go with us, do not bring us up from here." (Exodus 33:15), showing that he would rather be in the desert with God, than in the Promised Land without Him.

I mentioned Jackie Pullinger in Chapter 1: The Dynamics of Faith. In 1966, God told Jackie to get on a ship going around the world and not to get off until he told her. She got off in Hong Kong, and is still there today, sharing the love of Jesus.[1]

As Jesus Himself once said:

> "If anyone serves Me, let him follow Me; and where I am, there My servant will be also." (John 12:26)

You may not always feel like you know where you're going, but do you know who you're going with?

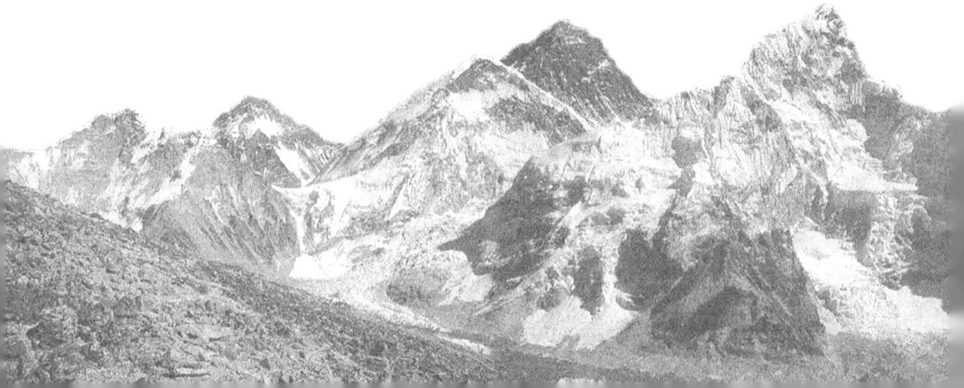

Chapter 4
BATTLESHIP TO GLORY, OR CARIBBEAN CRUISE?

By faith he dwelt in the land of promise as in a foreign country, dwelling in tents with Isaac and Jacob, the heirs with him of the same promise; for he waited for the city which has foundations, whose builder and maker is God.

These all died in faith, not having received the promises, but having seen them afar off were assured of them, embraced them and confessed that they were strangers and pilgrims on the earth. For those who say such things declare plainly that they seek a homeland.

But now they desire a better, that is, a heavenly country. Therefore God is not ashamed to be called their God, for He has prepared a city for them.

Hebrews 11:9, 10, 13, 14, 16

"THE MAN'S A DREAMER! GOOD! THAT PLACES him in close relationship to God. For down in the most wretched quarter of town God stands and dreams His dream; amid the grim, ensanguined battle wreckage; in the dim, cold twilights where old superstitions frown."

The man's a dreamer! The man in question? It was John Bunyan. The man who knew what it was like to "be a pilgrim." W. Burgess McCreary, in his biography of Bunyan, said, "If our young people will dream like Bunyan and serve like Bunyan, they will certainly reach the Celestial City and have the satisfaction of greeting multitudes of their fellow men who have followed in their train."[1] Oh, but how the gospel has changed. Do we still live as if we are just passing through this life, motivated by a heavenly hope, looking for a heavenly country, a city whose builder and maker is God? Is that what our friends see when they look at us? We sing about it at church, but are our values that much different from those of our non believing friends? Do we spend all our time, energy and money behaving as if this is the only life there is? Sadly, it would appear that all too often we do.

Do not hear me wrong. I am not advocating that we should "endure the misery of life" on our pilgrimage to heaven. No, not at all. Life is a gift from God, to be enjoyed as only a Christian can enjoy it. God has filled this world with many good things, which we should take time to savor. However, without God, what is the purpose of life? And this is the point: that for millions there is no purpose to life. Millions each year die in despair, without any hope at all. They do not know God! We do, and we have all eternity to spend with Him. How, then, can we not spend this life snatching others from the fire and saving them (Jude 23)? How can a doctor with an abundant supply of medicines spend all his time building a beautiful home instead of healing the sick? Why are we seemingly so unconcerned? What has gone wrong? What does it mean to live as a pilgrim today? It will mean making choices. Here are a few to think about.

Past or Present?

I have traveled to over sixty-five countries, and I see the same thing the world over. Many of us are living in the past. In one country I visited a famous mission that proudly declared they were keeping alive "old-time Christianity." Their services, however, were more like old-time music hall as they desperately sought to put on a show of what it was like in the good old days. Another time I visited a world-famous church which once used to shake with the power of God as literally thousands of sinners would come to hear God's redemptive message from the lips of His anointed servant. Today it seems more like a concert hall; a place to go to be entertained and reminded of the past. Oh, the tragedy of it all, and it's so unnecessary.

Perhaps Samuel Stevenson was reflecting on his visits to such places when he wrote these words:

> A city full of churches,
> Great preacher, lettered men,
> Grand music, choirs and organs;
> If these all fail, what then?
> Good workers, eager, earnest,
> Who labour hour by hour;
> But where, oh where, my brother,
> Is God's almighty power?
> Refinement: education!
> They want the very best.
> Their plans and schemes are perfect
> They give themselves no rest;
> They get the best of talent,
> They try their uttermost,
> But what they need, brother,
> Is God the Holy Ghost![2]

God once spoke through the prophet Isaiah saying, "Do not remember the former things, nor consider the things of old. Behold, I will do a new thing, now it shall spring forth; shall you not know it?" (Isaiah 43:18, 19a)

The pilgrim does not live in the past. He looks instead to the future, and this gives him strength to do great exploits in the present.

God's House or Ours?

> "Is it time for you yourselves to dwell in your paneled houses, and this temple to lie in ruins?" Now therefore, thus says the Lord of Hosts: "Consider your ways! You have sown much, and bring in little; you eat, but do not have enough; you drink, but you are not filled with drink; you clothe yourselves, but no one is warm; and he who earns wages, earns wages to put into a bag with holes." Thus says the Lord of Hosts: "Consider your ways!" (Haggai 1:4–7)

Do these words hit home? Are you more concerned about your own house than God's kingdom? Are you storing up treasures on earth instead of in heaven? If so, you know nothing of the joy of being a pilgrim.

I do not believe it is wrong for Christians to have money or to live in nice houses. However, it is so sad to see so many striving after these things as if their happiness and security were tied up in them. They are not. Only Jesus can satisfy our heart's desire, and only those who are totally surrendered to Him really know what it's like to be rich.

When I first went into missions, there were those who said to me, "You who go into missions need to understand that you wouldn't get anywhere if it wasn't for those of us who work to support you." I do not entirely agree with this, because it tends to make God smaller than He is. However, I have made one interesting observation. I know it is a generalization, but by and large I have discovered that people who say this type of thing are not those who are supporting missions! Most of them are too consumed with maintaining a standard of living way beyond what is adequate to be able to give to God's work. It surprised me to find out that much of the support for missions comes from the very poor—that's poor as the world sees it. Often other missionaries who live by faith are the most generous givers to missions—and the very rich, who have learned the secret of

Malachi 3:10. It is surprising how little support comes from those in the middle, who are working to better themselves in this life. What a tragedy this is, not only for missions, but also for the church and the individuals themselves.

Several times in the past, my wife and I have found that all our worldly possessions would fit into the back of a station wagon! It is nice not to be tied down by things. When God blesses me materially, and He often does, I give Him heartfelt thanks; when He doesn't, that's fine too. I know, like Paul, what it means to be content in all situations (Philippians 4:11).

Over the years I have stayed at some of the best hotels in the world, and on some of the hardest church floors; I have traveled in Southeast Asia by primitive dugout canoe and by expensive, modern speedboat; I have eaten in the best restaurants and in the poorest refugee camps; I have driven some of the world's greatest cars and some of its worst; I have lived in appalling conditions and in beautiful conditions. God has shown me that the more we are willing to give up, the more He compensates. I have no "visible" income, yet not even a top executive could buy the experiences I have had. And the best is yet to come!

The pilgrim will not settle for anything less than this reality. As Peter once said to Jesus, "See, we have left all and followed you." So He said to them, "Assuredly, I say to you, there is no one who has left house or parents or brothers or wife or children, for the sake of the kingdom of God, who shall not receive many times more in this present time, and in the age to come eternal life" (Luke 18:28–30).

The pilgrim builds for the life to come. He knows what he can take with him and what he can't. The only mansion he is interested in is the one being prepared for him in the city whose builder and maker is God.

Vision or Division?

John Bunyan was a dreamer and a pilgrim. We are often quick to mock those who stand out from the crowd. The term "idealist," instead of being a mark of virtue, has become somewhat derisory.

How sad that the idealism of youth soon gets replaced by the cynicism of middle age. John Bunyan may have had his head in the clouds, but his feet were planted firmly on the ground. For twelve years of his life they paced the cold, damp floor of Bedford Jail. His crime? Refusing to stop preaching the gospel.

Throughout history, the men and women of God who have made an impact for the kingdom have been people who "swam against the tide," who "went against the grain." We owe them a great debt.

"I had a dream today," said Martin Luther King. And then he was gone; robbed of life by an assassin's bullet. As Hebrews 11:13 says, "These all died in faith, not having received the promises." They were those "of whom the world was not worthy" (Hebrews 11:38a). In Catherine Marshall's book *Beyond Our Selves*, she devotes a whole chapter to "the prayer that makes your dreams come true."[3] Does it all sound a bit fanciful? Are we above that kind of thing in these enlightened times? There is a definite correlation between dreaming and the pilgrim life. Only those who can see clearly with the eyes of faith the life that lies beyond the grave can have the confidence and courage not to make their home in this world. And vision is essential for unity.

I was apprehensive about leading an interdenominational mission. How would we all get on together? How would Pentecostals, Baptists, Brethren, Anglicans, and a whole range of others ever work together without disagreement? I discovered an interesting point. When we were out on the field working toward a goal, we never had a single problem. The only time there was ever any tension was when we would go on a retreat. Then we would turn in on ourselves and the differences became more apparent. You see, whenever the people of God stand still and lose their vision, disunity creeps in. It's time to start dreaming again, like Martin Luther King.

I believe God has a dream today. I believe He dreams of the day when His people will stop arguing over Him and start taking Him at His word.

In Acts 1:8, Jesus said, "But you shall receive power when the Holy Spirit has come upon you." Power to do what, you might ask?

Is it power to show off with, or power to turn the church into a circus act? No, let's read on: "And you shall be witnesses to Me in Jerusalem, and in all Judea and Samaria, and to the end of the earth."

Personally, I have lost count of the number of times I've heard people pray for the power of the Holy Spirit, but I can count on one hand the times I've heard someone pray that they might become a witness "to the end of the earth." God's dream is that we will stop all this nonsense. We don't need power unless we are going to be obedient. In Acts 5:32 we are told that God gives the Holy Spirit to those who are obedient. So perhaps we should stop praying if we've no intention of obeying!

I believe God has a dream today. I believe He dreams of the day when Christians will stop using the sword of the Spirit (Ephesians 6:17) to carve each other up, and instead use it to launch the attack on Satan and the evil which threatens to devour and destroy humankind. God dreams that we will begin to understand that "walking in the footsteps of Jesus" means more than a trip to the Holy Land. God dreams of the day when we will stop playing games and enlist in the army. God dreams of the day His people will stop feeling so at home in this world, as they capture a vision for spending eternity with Him.

There was a time in the late eighteenth century when a young man working all alone at his workbench had a dream. By his bench was an open Bible and on the wall a crude map of the world that he had made himself. He dreamed of taking the gospel to the millions who had never heard. But what could one man, a mere cobbler, do? His enthusiasm, however, was infectious, and it wasn't long before speaking engagements came his way.

Then on May 30, 1792, William Carey delivered his now famous sermon at a meeting in Nottingham, in the East Midlands of England. His appeal was fervent, and he made a profound impression on his hearers. The core of his message was captured in the ringing words, "Expect great things from God. Attempt great things for God." At last his vision took hold. Others were now fired up too, and the first modern missionary society came into being. Through the Baptist Missionary Society, the dreams of a cobbler became a reality in India.[4]

Let them call us dreamers, visionaries, idealists if they wish. Don't they know that without vision the people perish (Proverbs 29:18)? And don't they know that it's God's will that none should perish (2 Peter 3:9)? It's time to put the picnic things away and join the pilgrimage. Islam is on the march; apathy is on the march; materialism is on the march; fascism is on the march. It's time for the mighty army of God to rise up and go into battle. Time is running out. Jesus said, "I must work the works of Him who sent Me while it is day; the night is coming when no one can work" (John 9:4). Are you ready and armed to go into battle to the ends of the earth? Wake up! This is no time to be complacent. Let's unite. We cannot lose. God has called us to pilgrimage; He has given us His Holy Spirit and His promises. Tear up the cruise line ticket; your ship has already come in, and it's gray with bold black letters on it. Didn't you know? There's a war on.

Chapter 5
No Turning Back

And truly if they had called to mind that country from which they had come out, they would have had opportunity to return.

Hebrews 11:15

It is not uncommon for a convict, upon release from prison, to immediately commit a crime and be thrown back in jail. Ask a prison warden and he'll tell you, "Well, he couldn't cope with freedom, could he? He feels safe and secure in here." As incredible as this may seem, I shouldn't think it surprises any of us that much, for it is only an extreme example of a basic human trait familiar to many of us.

You've heard it said, "Better the devil you know than one you don't know," but who says that the devil you don't know is a devil at all? Perhaps the expression itself gives us a clue to the answer. "Out of the frying pan, into the fire," is another well-known and extremely negative cliché that we clutch to our bosom and cherish. Oh, how we love to listen to the father of lies! Listen instead to the words of Him who is the truth:

"For I know the thoughts that I think toward you," says the Lord, "thoughts of peace and not of evil, to give you a future and a hope." (Jeremiah 29:11)

Only a Fool Would Go Back to Egypt

God had told them, you know. There was no excuse. His exact words were that it was "a land flowing with milk and honey" (Exodus 3:17). That couldn't be clearer, could it? It was a good land that He was leading them to. His plans for them were good; He was going to give them a future and a hope, but they threw it all away. Just like the convict on parole, they too wanted to be "thrown back inside" at the earliest opportunity.

God had already worked the miraculous by bringing them out of Egypt and across the dry bed of the Red Sea, and yet still they doubted. How they must have worn Moses down. They never stopped complaining, "We wanna go back to Egypt."

They remind me of a story I once heard about a monk who had joined a silent order in an isolated part of the countryside. The rules were that monks kept silence for two years, after which they could speak two words. This was followed by a further two years of silence and then another two words. After the first two years were up, the monk appeared before his superior, who said, "Well, what have you to say?" "Bed hard," replied the monk. Another two years of silence followed, and then it was time for another two words. "Well, brother?" "Food bad," was the reply. Finally, after the third period of two years' silence, the monk took advantage of his two-word opportunity to say, "I quit!" The superior clenched his fists and said, "I'm not surprised. All you've done since you came here is complain, complain, complain."

I'm not sure whether at this point Moses would have appreciated that funny little story, for his complaining followers never kept even two minutes of silence, never mind two years! They had worn him down to the point where his sense of humor, along with his clarity of thought and faith in God, seemed to have evaporated.

The negative spirit that pervaded the camp was obviously infectious; fear and unbelief won the day.

How many great projects, inspired of the Holy Spirit, have been nipped in the bud because the weary leader, the tired pastor, finally gave in to the negative voices around him? "You know where this is going to lead us, don't you, Pastor?—bankruptcy. Mark my words. I've been in this church fifty years, and now you're putting everything we've built at risk. And for what? What are you trying to prove, Pastor?" And so the kingdom of God, having taken a step forward, must now take two steps back.

Since I've been in ministry, I've lost count of the number of times I've heard comments like, "Oh, you'll never find anywhere to live," or "You're not going there, are you? It's dangerous there, people get mugged all the time." Once when we were about to board a train in Bangkok, Thailand, for the three-day journey to Singapore, someone said, "Oh, you shouldn't go by train. It's full of cockroaches, and it's always being attacked by communist bandits in remote areas of the jungle." If we had listened to these "comforting" words, we may have ended up missing one of the most exciting and interesting journeys of our lives!

We need to realize the danger in always looking back. God has warned us that if we keep recalling to mind that which He has brought us out of, we will have opportunity to return. We will be like those who had little, and even what they had was taken away (Matthew 13:12). God is not pleased with those who draw back (Hebrews 10:39). Indeed, only a fool would go back to Egypt!

How to Look Down on Giants

It's important to realize that unbelief often leads to exaggeration and a distortion of the truth. Satan is the author of all lies, and we need to discern between the caution that comes from wisdom and the fear that comes from unbelief.

So the spies went into Canaan to check it out. "Sure, God has told us that it's a land of milk and honey, but maybe there are other things about the place He neglected to tell us. There's got to be a catch somewhere, hasn't there? I mean, we can't just walk in there as if we owned the place. It might be a trap." Sure enough, their fears proved to be well founded. It wasn't long before they were hightailing it back to Moses. "Moses, Moses, we must get out of here. We can't go in, Moses, we can't. There are g-g-g-g-giants in the land, Moses. It's impossible. What will we do?" Moses just stood there. He was too tired to speak. Eventually it was Caleb who broke the silence. He was one of the spies himself. He'd seen those so-called giants too. "Okay, guys, calm yourselves down now. Don't go getting yourselves all excited. Aren't you forgetting something? I suggest we immediately go up and take possession of the land, for we are well able to overcome it."

They must have stood gaping at Caleb with open mouths. "Cocky young fellow, isn't he?" "Pretty full of himself, don't you think?" But Caleb was not full of himself at all; he was full of the Holy Spirit, and full of faith. He remembered the awesome power of God that he had seen displayed so many times, and he knew God as Father.

What would a child walking with his father do if they came across giants? Why, he would jump up on his dad's shoulders, wouldn't he? "Give me a piggyback, Dad! Let me up." Once on top of his dad's shoulders, he wouldn't be so frightened. From such a vantage point he would be able to see everything in its proper perspective. He would be amazed to find himself not looking up at the giants, but looking down on them. "Hey, you guys, you don't look so big after all. Out of my way, I'm coming through."

So it is with us. What are the giants that threaten to hinder your progress? Fear of criticism, rejection or failure? Concern about finances, or where you will live? Jump up onto the shoulders of your heavenly Father. Then you'll see things in perspective. The giants aren't half as big from up there.

The Man or Woman God Uses

Watching a cartoon in a cold, dark church in Southend, a seaside town in the east of England, is hardly the time to have an encounter with God, but that's what happened to me. However, the cartoon was *The Lion, the Witch, and the Wardrobe* by C. S. Lewis. If you've seen it, then perhaps you'll remember the part where Aslan, the lion representing Christ, is going up a long hill on his way to be sacrificed on behalf of the others. On and on he walks up that lonely hill for what seems like an eternity. It's difficult for me to try to express in writing how God used that incident to speak to me. All I know is that it was as if God was saying over and over, "This is what I want—follow me." I think I had some kind of supernatural revelation of the complete and utter loneliness and rejection that Christ experienced at Calvary. I had been going through a rough time in my ministry. Many people had misunderstood what I was trying to do and why. This had come as a great shock to me, for I was naive. Many times I felt like giving up, and it had never occurred to me that I had somehow entered into His sufferings. This and much more was what it meant to be a disciple, a follower of Jesus Christ. As Jesus Himself said when referring to His coming crucifixion:

> Unless a grain of wheat falls into the ground and dies, it remains alone; but if it dies, it produces much grain.
>
> He who loves his life will lose it, and he who hates his life in this world will keep it for eternal life. If anyone serves Me, let him follow Me; and where I am, there My servant will be also. (John 12:24-26)

And where was Jesus? He was on His way to be crucified. It had taken a cartoon to bring home to me the full impact of what Christ did on the cross and what He requires of us. With tears streaming down my face, I rededicated my life to following Him, whatever the cost.

Not, you understand, that the cost is not more than fully compensated for by the sheer joy of communion with Christ and by more blessings than we can begin to imagine. After all, it was Caleb who eventually entered the Promised Land, with Joshua, and received all that God had promised. We don't give things up unless there is something better to replace them. Mahatma Gandhi realized this when he said, "Only give up a thing when you want some other condition so much that the thing no longer has any attraction for you, or when it seems to interfere with that which is more greatly desired."[1]

You see, it's like a young married couple expecting their first child. They worry, perhaps, about losing their freedom. No longer will they be able to go out just when they want. Yet when the baby comes, all those things are forgotten. Something much more wonderful has taken their place.

What are you going to settle for—being one of the crowd, or a follower of Jesus? Not that there aren't millions following Him today with whom you can find fellowship. But you had better believe that, if you do decide to follow Him completely, it will get you into trouble both inside the church and outside it. Are you ready for that?

Caleb followed the Lord wholeheartedly. God tells us that he ran on a different fuel than the others; he had a different spirit in him (Numbers 14:24). Can He say that of you and me?

Corrie Ten Boom has said, "I like so very much to pray with an open Bible. I like to say, 'Father, you have said it, now you must do it!' And God likes that—for God has meant every promise of the Bible and God likes it when you mean business with His promises."[2] That's the spirit that Caleb had—a complete and utter trust in his God, like that of a child in his father. These are the men and women that God can use.

We had only been "living by faith," as the saying goes, for a few weeks, and we desperately needed five hundred pounds. Until that time the largest gift we had received had been fifty pounds, so this was a lot of money to us. We needed it within a week. Nobody knew but those on our team, all of whom had agreed to talk to no one about the need except God. All week we prayed, and nothing came. Then the seventh day arrived. If it didn't come that day, it would be too late! Sure enough, the first post brought with it a check for five hundred pounds. The person who sent it had no idea at all that it was needed. Since then I have seen God do the same thing, on an even bigger scale, more times than I can remember. God likes it when we mean business with His promises.

I was reminded of this once on a visit to Chicago for a week's evangelism. At Moody Bible Institute, I noticed a huge picture on the wall. It showed the original school building, and on the painting was a quote from D. L. Moody: "This looks like a fine building for a school. Let's ask the Lord to give it to us." This is what they did, and sure enough, God delivered it into their hands.

Consider for a moment just how much this one statement of Jesus would revolutionize your life, if only you believed it: "If you ask anything in My name, I will do it" (John 14:14). Stop and think about that. What does it really mean? Too simple? Too good to be true? What's the catch? Sounds a bit extreme, perhaps? Well, I didn't say it—Jesus did! He said this or something very similar twice in John chapter 14, twice in chapter 15 and twice in chapter 16. He wanted us to understand!

You see, these are the people that God is looking for—people of commitment and people of faith. These are the ones He can use—not those who argue and debate, but those who believe and act. He wants people of faith who will not keep looking back but who will move ahead with confidence in His promises. And He's not standing aloof and watching us make fools of ourselves, either. As soon as we step out in faith to trust Him, He immediately joins with us. He works with us in a partnership. As it says in 2 Chronicles 16:9:

> For the eyes of the Lord run to and fro throughout the whole earth, to show Himself strong on behalf of those whose heart is loyal to Him.

The question we must answer is this: do those eyes stop when they see us, or do they just pass over?

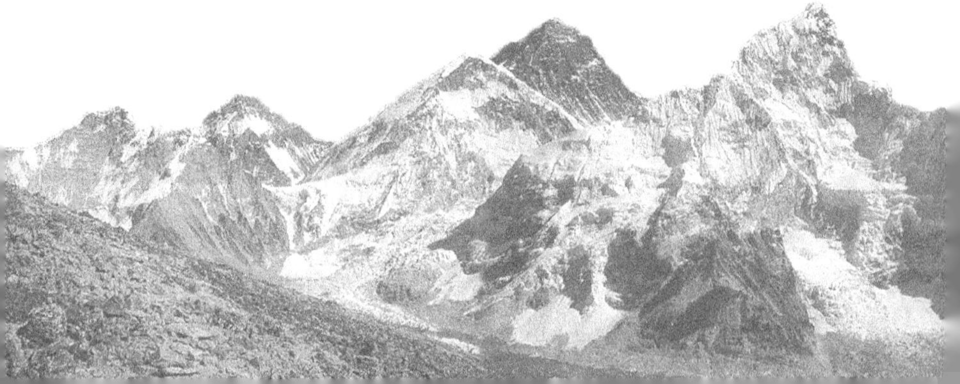

Chapter 6
ME AND MY BOY

By faith Abraham, when he was tested, offered up Isaac, and he who had received the promises offered up his only begotten son.

Hebrews 11:17

A YOUNG CHILD WAS FALLING DOWN A SNOWY mountain slope in Switzerland toward a sheer drop of several thousand feet. Everyone watched, dumbfounded. Nobody could move. Then suddenly there was a man charging through the snow toward the precipice, trying to intercept the child. Everyone stopped breathing; nobody believed that another human being could move at such a speed. The man seemed unafraid of the obvious danger he was in. Sure enough, a miracle happened—the man reached the child just in time, and somehow managed to save the child and himself. Nobody had ever witnessed such courage. Later on, as everyone was complimenting the man, someone said, "Didn't you realize that you could have been killed?" "I didn't care," answered the man. "You see, that was my son!"

The Bible says, "Greater love has no one than this, than to lay down one's life for his friends" (John 15:13). And it's also true that there is no greater love than that of a father and mother for their child. A father would rather die himself than allow his son or daughter to die. Imagine then the anguish of one who knows that his son is going to die, and that he will be the one to bring it about.

You are perhaps familiar with the concept of "climbing Mount Moriah" and "laying your Isaac on the altar." There has hardly been a man or woman of God who, in the early years of ministry, didn't have to come to a point of relinquishment. He would have to allow his ministry, his dreams and his ambitions to die, only to have them resurrected by God when he had learned the lesson of putting Him first. The account of Abraham and Isaac demonstrates this principle well. However, there is another important point in this story, one we are apt to miss if we are not careful.

Perhaps you have heard it said that we should never ask someone else to do that which we are not willing to do ourselves. It is a good principle. When God sent Abraham up the mountain to sacrifice his son, He knew the anguish and heartache that Abraham felt. God was not asking Abraham to do something that He wouldn't do. God intended to sacrifice His son, too! Unlike Isaac, however, there would be no last-minute reprieve for Jesus. When we read the account of Abraham and Isaac from this angle, how can we get to the end without weeping? Let's hear it from Abraham's viewpoint.

I'll Never Forget That Day (Genesis 22:1–19)

I just couldn't believe it. It didn't make any sense. There I was, sojourning in the land of the Philistines, minding my own business, when I heard a voice.

"Abraham!"

I nearly jumped out of my skin. I knew it was Him. "Here I am," I replied.

"Take now your son, your only son Isaac, whom you love, and go to the land of Moriah, and offer him there as a burnt offering on one of the mountains of which I shall tell you."

I was lost for words. I didn't doubt for one moment that it was God who had spoken, but it was so totally out of character. "God's not like that," I said to myself again and again. It just didn't make any sense. *Oh no, Lord. Please, no, not Isaac. Anything, Lord, but not Isaac.* My thoughts were all confused. I didn't know what to do, who to turn to.

My mind went back all those years to the time when God had first promised us a son. I was ninety-nine years old and was then called Abram, but God told me to change my name. He said that I would be the father of many nations, and that's what my new name means: "father of a multitude." God promised that He would give me a land, a special land, and that through me all the nations would be blessed. It was all a little overwhelming at the time. My wife had to change her name, too; she became Sarah, which means "princess." Then we knew that we must be dreaming, because God said that I would have a son by Sarah. At that point I just burst out laughing. I fell on the floor and rolled about. *How can a hundred-year-old man and a ninety-year-old woman have a child?* I thought. Surely He was talking about Ishmael, my other son by Hagar. But no, He wasn't, that wouldn't be acceptable. This son had to be by Sarah.

Suddenly I felt convicted. I now believed that God would honor His promise. It was foolish to laugh at Him like that. Sarah laughed, too, when she found out, but God reminded us of an important fact that I had forgotten. He said, "Is anything too hard for the Lord?" Of course I knew the truth of that statement in my mind, but somehow I had always thought that it was only true when it applied to someone else; it couldn't be true for me. How wrong I was. I no longer doubted that God would do what He said He would.

And He did! When I was one hundred years old I became the father of Isaac, whose name means "laughter." This time we really did have something to laugh about. Sarah and I felt like dancing around the room, laughing and praising God.

The years that followed were tremendous. Isaac was everything a father could want in a son. We did everything together. We would go on fishing trips and talk all day till the sun went down. We would go on long hikes together. We had all kinds of family games that we used to play; hide-and-seek was one of our favorites. Young Isaac used to hide in the most incredible places; it was almost impossible to ever find him. We were so happy.

And now this. Surely God didn't really want me to sacrifice Isaac. What would be the point of it all, after everything that had happened and all that we had been through? I never slept at all that night. I spent the night pacing up and down the room, or just lying prostrate on the floor before God. "Oh, God," I cried, "please take this whole mess away. Oh, please, Lord! Yet not my will be done, but Yours."

When God speaks I believe that you must obey, whatever it is He asks of you. And somehow I knew that I would have to muster up the strength to go through with it. Yet I would still hope and pray. "Lord, I am just an old man. Take me, I beg of you, but please, spare Isaac."

We had an early breakfast the next morning. It was a long journey to Mount Moriah, and I knew we would have to set off early.

"Isaac, be a good lad, will you, and go saddle the donkeys for us."

"Oh, great, Dad, where are we going? Are you taking me fishing again?" It was almost more than I could bear. It took us three days to get to Mount Moriah, yet Isaac and I hardly spoke to each other all the way. I knew he sensed that there was something going on.

When we arrived, I unloaded the wood I had brought along and picked up the knife. Then we set off on the long trek up the mountain.

"Dad, where are we going? What's the wood for?"

"Let's not talk just now, son." I felt a lump in my throat. All the time I was quietly praying, "Lord, what's this all about? Please, Lord, is there not some other way? Yet not my will, but Thine."

"Dad?"

"Yes, son?"

"Are we going to make an offering to the Lord?"

"Yes, son, that's what the wood and the fire are for."

"But where is the lamb for the burnt offering, Dad?"

"God will provide the lamb, my son; God will provide."

I saw the top of the mountain getting nearer, and I tried to walk more slowly, but it was no use; we were there. I don't know how to describe to you the pain and anguish of my soul at that time. Isaac was just looking up at me and smiling. He trusted me so much.

"Lord, why Isaac? What has he ever done wrong? Nothing, Lord, he's done nothing. We are putting an innocent person to death here, Lord. Why should someone who is innocent die? I don't understand.

It's not fair." By this time, I was just feeling numb. I worked matter-of-factly, building the altar; I didn't dare look at Isaac in case I broke down.

The time had come. I just gently picked Isaac up in my arms and laid him on the altar. He was smiling; his eyes were so happy. He thought we were playing a game. He trusted me so much. I quickly bound him hand and foot and reached for the knife. Never in a million years had I expected God to put my faith to the test like this. Could I go through with it? Slowly, I lifted the knife into the air. My eyes were so wet that Isaac was just a blur. He was giggling; he still thought it was a game. I closed my eyes and counted to three.

One...

Two...

"ABRAHAM!"

"Aaarrgh!"

"ABRAHAM!"

"Yes? Yes, what is it? Here I am."

"Do not lay your hand on the lad, or do anything to him; for now I know that you fear God, since you have not withheld your son, your only son, from Me."

I dropped the knife and just stood there. You could see I was visibly shaking. Then I noticed a ram caught in the thicket! I quickly substituted the ram for Isaac, and together we offered it up as a burnt offering to God. I shall never forget that day.

Unless you've been through it, you can't imagine what it is like, putting your own innocent child to death. It was an absolute nightmare—my darkest hour.

> Now it was about the sixth hour, and there was darkness over all the earth until the ninth hour. Then the sun was darkened, and the veil of the temple was torn in two. And when Jesus had cried out with a loud voice, He said, "Father, into your hands I commit My spirit." Having said this, He breathed His last (Luke 23:44–46).

I wonder how God felt at that moment?

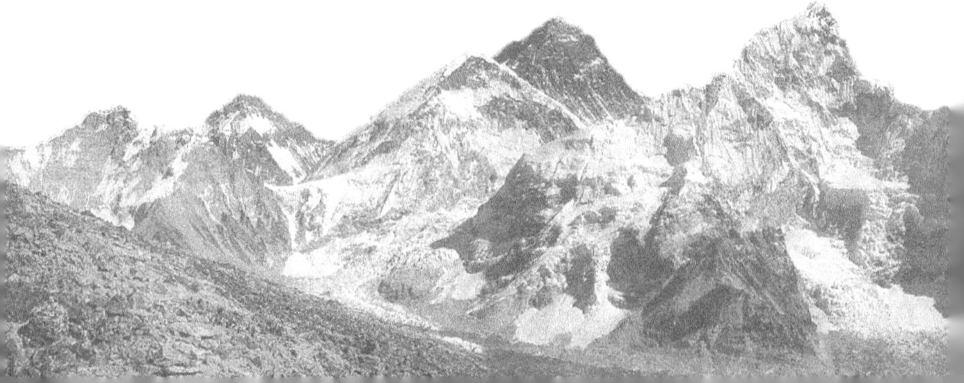

Chapter 7
YOU CALL THIS A CHRISTIAN FAMILY?

By faith Isaac blessed Jacob and Esau concerning things to come. By faith Jacob, when he was dying, blessed each of the sons of Joseph, and worshiped, leaning on the top of his staff. By faith Joseph, when he was dying, made mention of the departure of the children of Israel, and gave instructions concerning his bones.

Hebrews 11:20–22

DO YOU COME FROM A GOOD, SOLID, HAPPY home? If you do, then according to statistics you are the exception, not the rule. The chances are that your background has had its fair share of hurts and problems. Perhaps you despair about the future. You know God can save you, but you want more, and rightly so. You want Him to use you to further His kingdom. You want to live a life of faith, to make your life count, but too many hurts from the past seem to be holding you back. Do not give up hope.

Consider the family that Jesus Himself descended from. The accounts of Isaac, Jacob, Esau, Joseph, and their whole family would make an excellent script for any television soap opera! You couldn't find a more scheming, conniving, backstabbing bunch than these.

Yet God used them and worked through them. Why? Because He is the God who heals, who restores, and who redeems. No person or situation is beyond His redemption. He has saved you, and He wants to use you.

Love Finds a Way

This is how God salvaged the marriage of one friend of mine, who has now gone on to become a Christian leader. I will let him tell his own story.

I was born to godly parents, and church was always important to my family. The only time I can remember missing a Sunday service was when we were snowbound on our little farm in South Dakota. I was always active in church, and in Sunday school I was a favorite. My mother was Sunday School Superintendent for many years, so I had certain standards to live up to. I learned how to be "religious," and I found that I was quite good at it. In my confirmation class I was the first one, and maybe the only one, to get one hundred percent on every weekly test for all three years of confirmation preparation. I was president of the church youth group, appointed to a special committee to represent the youth of the church, and even elected to represent the area at the District Youth Association. I had learned my lessons well—I was good at "religion!"

But God doesn't have any grandchildren—He only has children, a fresh batch every generation. Just because my parents were godly didn't automatically mean that I would be. I had to decide to be a child of God, otherwise I would remain a "grandchild" and nothing more.

I didn't consciously decide to depart from what I had been taught. It just started with a thought; a "What if . . . ?" or "I bet it would be fun. . ." Just a fleeting thought captured for a moment to examine and then to dwell on. God's Word is true. I can testify to that, for His Word says, "For as he thinketh in his heart, so is he" (Proverbs 23:7). That is exactly what began to happen. I began to experiment with little things, nothing big, mind you, nothing that was actually harmful, just little things. And when the little things were not "really" hurting me, I began to think of other things. I began to drift, to defect from the kingdom of God, to that garden of pleasure and delight at whose gate I had stood but which I had never entered.

I wasn't a wild kid! No, no; I was reasonable, responsible and a model youth; at least to those people to whom it was important to be thought of as such! I continued practicing "religion." I worked as a counselor and program director at a Bible camp for five summers. I had a good deal of command of the Bible, and I had some teachers who began to tell me how this book was up for a certain amount of interpretation! Things had changed, they told me—customs, language, clothing, circumstances—and things that were meant one way when they were written did not necessarily mean the same thing today. One of my favorite verses was 1 Corinthians 6:12, at least the first part of the verse: "All things are lawful . . ." The part about not all things being expedient was sort of lost in the translation. One of my favorite "sports" was to get together with a couple of the counselors, get a couple of six-packs of beer, and sit around discussing theology. I was doing what Paul talks about in 2 Timothy 3:5: I was practicing a form of godliness but denying its power; I was planting one foot firmly in the world.

College served to reinforce the style of life I was choosing. While active in the student Christian Association, I was also active in drinking and rebellious behavior. When it came time to graduate and begin my career, the logical step was to get married. I was attracted to my wife, but I needed her more in order to fit the role of the young teacher! By that time, my thoughts had become my actions. I had now turned my back on the garden fence and had begun to wander away.

I went to work and quickly established myself as an active and willing member of a local church and of the world. As a man who was game to do almost anything, I was into drinking, partying and having fun. I had control, or so I thought, over my destiny, my life, my world. I had one foot solidly in the world, but it's hard to stand in shifting sand. My world began to fall apart. My actions gradually became more bizarre. The defection was becoming more evident.

Drugs, alcohol, pornography, abusive behavior, sexual experimentation, blasphemy—there was nothing which seemed wrong or out of the ordinary. My actions had become my habits.

My wife and I were drifting apart. That's not entirely correct—we didn't drift, we were speeding apart in different directions. After five years of teaching, we decided to make a move and go back to school. Back in college at an older age was quite different. I began to be an influence on many of the students, and I am ashamed to say, not a very good one. I was no longer interested in "playing religion." I was not interested in anything which had to do with God. I had not only defected from the kingdom, but I had begun to be an advocate for the other side. My habits had become my character.

After a few years in school, my wife and I took a position as group home parents for court-referred juvenile delinquents. On the outside we were doing well—on the inside I was in control of a disaster. We were divorced in practice if not in law. We were sharing the same house but living two separate lives. Both my wife and I had a succession of lovers. My character was becoming my destiny.

I have always enjoyed reading. Whenever I wanted to take my mind off a problem, reading was just the remedy. I began to read, and one day on a whim I decided to read my confirmation Bible. It was a dandy Bible. It was as good as the day I got it. It even cracked when I opened it. I began to look forward to my time reading the Bible, and I would get up early in the morning to read. One day I was listening to a tape which someone had given to me, and the speaker read and talked about Deuteronomy 11:10: "For the land, whither thou goest in to possess it, is not as the land of Egypt, from whence ye came out, where thou sowed thy seed and watered it with thy foot, as a garden of herbs" (KJV). I began to realize that just as the children of Israel had used their feet to open and close the earthen irrigation gates and had thereby controlled the water and their very existence, so I had been watering with my feet and had been attempting to control my destiny. Then something strange and wonderful began to happen. I began to talk with God. I wasn't back in the garden, but the Holy Spirit had drawn me back to the fence, and I was looking over it, looking for God.

"Lord, I know quite a lot about you. I have been taught a lot of religion and Bible; I know about you and your Jesus. I know what men say about Jesus. He was a prophet, teacher, healer, magician, God (although I never understood that one), and a culturally significant personage (that's a good one, isn't it?); but I still don't quite understand how it all fits together."

Then one morning, sitting in the kitchen, I "randomly" turned to Matthew 16:13–15, the story of when Jesus came to Caesarea Philippi and asked His disciples, "Who do men say that I am?" They told him, "Well, some folks say that you're Elijah, some say Jeremiah or one of the prophets." Then Jesus said, "But what about you? Who do you say that I am?" That question came off the page, shot through my mind, past my reason, past my logic, right straight into my heart, and there it exploded! Jesus was asking me that same question, "Who do you say that I am?" And right then I could see. The Holy Spirit revealed Jesus to me, and I answered with Peter, "You are the Christ, the Son of the Living God." At that moment I saw what had happened. I had defected from the kingdom more by default than by anything else. My thoughts had become actions; my actions, habits; my habits, characteristics; and my characteristics, my destiny.

As I see the beginning from the end, I see that indeed my story is not that unique. In fact, Christianity itself has wandered away from the garden through the same process of thought to action, to habit, to characteristic, to destiny. Maybe you have, too. Maybe you are somewhere in that vicious circle today. If you are, let me testify to you that the one and only way to break the circle is to look at the second part of 2 Timothy 3:5: ". . . the power thereof." Don't deny the power of Jesus. Just as the Holy Spirit revealed Jesus to Peter, to me and to countless others through the ages, He can do it for you. He is the same Spirit. He is not limited by time, changing language, customs, clothing or circumstances. The same principle works—the individual and personal experience of Jesus, revealed by the Holy Spirit, acknowledged and confessed in the one true, unchanging rock; the life-changing power of Jesus.

And by the way, when the Holy Spirit was leading me back to the garden fence and around to the gate, He had been on the other side of the garden leading my wife in the same way. When I came in through the gate, who should I find kneeling in the vegetables, but the very woman God had given to me as a helpmate so many years before, even though I didn't know it then. Now I thank the Lord that I have the most beautiful wife in the world.

Jesus wants to change your life, rebuild your marriage, your family, your home. He did it for me, and He can do it for you.

In 1 Corinthians 13, that famous "love chapter," we are told that love never fails; it bears all things, believes all things, hopes all things, endures all things. You see human wisdom, the wisdom of this world, will say, "Cut your losses and run," but that is not God's way. Love always hopes. Love will find a way. To give up hope is literally to deny the faith. It is saying, "God cannot do it," when the reality is not only that God can do it, but that He actually wants to do it even more than we do.

It is not without reason that Jesus was descended from a line of ordinary people with ordinary problems. Nor is it insignificant that He chose ordinary men as His disciples. The strength of God is made perfect in weakness (2 Corinthians 12:9). God has chosen the foolish things of this world to put to shame the wise (1 Corinthians 1:27). Our gospel is not a gospel of good people being religious, but a gospel of power as the Savior reaches down into the gutter of life and rescues sinners from hell.

There is nothing in the world more powerful than love, because God is love (1 John 4:8). One aspect of that love is forgiveness. Because God is all-powerful, all-loving, all-forgiving, there is hope for all humankind. And if we are willing to take on the nature of God by surrendering to the Lordship of Christ, then there is hope too for families and relationships that have been torn apart through bitterness.

The Power of Forgiveness

Now Isaac blessed Jacob and Esau concerning things to come, but this was no ordinary blessing. The whole episode was characterized by greed, treachery, deceit and every manner of sin. Jacob exploited his brother's weakness for food and took his birthright. Esau so easily forsook the spiritual for the carnal. Rebekah, their mother, encouraged Jacob to trick his father, her husband, into passing on the blessing to him. What a family! Though it would seem to me that Isaac, perhaps, wasn't completely taken in by all this (see Genesis 27:21). I suspect that he had a shrewd idea that he was blessing Jacob, not Esau. Normally Jacob would never be allowed to get away with this, but Isaac and Rebekah had already been told by God that they would give birth to twins, who would represent two nations, and that the older one would serve the younger. Esau was born first and normally would have received the blessing, but to fulfil Scripture, this time it had to be the other way around. So by faith, that is, believing God knew what He was doing even though he didn't understand it all, Isaac blessed Jacob.

Esau was understandably bitter toward Jacob. He decided that after an acceptable time of mourning for Isaac after his death (because like all good religious people he was concerned about what others would think), he would go after Jacob and kill him.

Jacob, however, fled to Haran where he got involved in more dubious activity with Leah, Rachel, and their maids. His years with Leah and Rachel seemed to consist of little more than jumping in and out of bed with first one and then the other, then one maid, then the other maid. Again, the whole episode was full of lies, deceit and trickery, yet it was from all this that we got the twelve tribes of Israel! God obviously did not approve of all that happened, yet He was still at work in the midst of it.

Then the time came for Jacob to meet with his brother Esau again; and understandably he was afraid. He even tried to buy his way out of trouble. He needn't have worried, though, for Esau was pleased to see him, running out to meet and embrace him. Instead of continuing to harbor resentment and bitterness, Esau chose to forgive. We should remember that Christian behavior is not confined exclusively to believers. God is at work in all the world, not just in the church.

The act of forgiveness does not come easily. It is right that it should be that way. It is something we need to draw on God's strength to help us do. Yet forgiveness is one of the most powerful forces in the world today. I remember visiting a Vietnamese family in Toronto, Canada, who knew of a certain injustice that I had suffered from some people back in England. Curiously, they enquired after those people, watching my reaction all the time. I was able to tell them quite sincerely that the people were well and that we still spent a lot of time together and were the best of friends. They literally could not believe it. "How can you still be friends after what they did to you?" Despite being very religious, their response was that I should have taken revenge. The whole concept of forgiveness was just too much for them. I think this testimony had more impact on them than any evangelistic message I might have been able to bring, for forgiveness is the gospel in action.

"Ah," I hear you say, "but what about justice?" Remember, though, that it is up to God to judge, not us. And are we really that concerned about justice? Was it just that Jesus should die on a cross for our sins? Do we deserve to go to heaven? No. Do not be deceived; it is not concern for justice that stops us forgiving, rather it is the desire for vindication and, yes, even revenge. But be warned: if we take that route, we will only end up destroying ourselves, as the words of Steve and Annie Chapman's song illustrate so well:

> *Two Children*
> Two children, a brother and a sister,
> Born to a father who was a slave to wine,
> They do remember their younger years of sorrow,
> How their Daddy used to hurt them time after time.
> But somehow they grew to be so different,
> Their lives turned out to be like day and night.
> One lives in peace up in Ohio,
> One was full of hate until she died.

I wondered what could make the difference in the two of them.
Both had reasons to be bitter,
But one was so sweet.
How could one live in peace and not the other?

Not long ago the answer came clear to me.
I saw the brother at his Daddy's grave
Placing flowers there, his eyes were filled with tears
As he said, "Daddy, once again I do forgive you
For the way you made us suffer through the years."

Now I can see how the two could be so different,
How their hearts turned out to be like day and night.
He lives in peace up in Ohio,
She was bitter 'til the day she died.
He lives in forgiveness up in Ohio,
She was bitter 'til the day she died.
A bitter heart was the reason she died.[1]

Early Retirement? No Thanks!

Every family has its old folks; they may be grandparents or aunties and uncles. Usually they are very popular, at least with the children, but are they taken seriously? Society would tell us that the world belongs to the young, and that older people should move over. God's pattern, however, is that the world belongs to Him, and is given to us to manage. He expects old and young to work together. Why? Because we need each other. Many a man or woman of God has proved to be the most fruitful for the kingdom in the last years of their life. Isaac, Jacob and Joseph were no exception. Though they did many things, they are remembered in Hebrews 11 for those great acts of faith in the closing moments of their lives. It is never too late to act in faith.

I remember a church deacon who had just visited a dying old lady, not a believer, saying, "She was so worried about sin in her life. She kept saying, 'I'm not ready to meet God.' I said to her, 'Nonsense, you've led a good life. If anyone's led a good life, you have!'" I couldn't believe it. How frustrating. This well-meaning deacon had sought to be kind, but instead of offering false comfort, he should have led her to Christ. Right then she needed her Savior, not pious platitudes. It is never too late to take a step of faith.

By faith Jacob blessed Joseph and his sons, and even while he was dying, worshiped his God. Jacob did not expect to be able to see Ephraim and Manasseh, due to his blindness; however, God stepped in and supernaturally gave him a glimpse of them.

Today, passing on an inheritance to our offspring is supposed to involve money and material goods, but such an inheritance is of no value at all compared to what we could be leaving our children. Jacob reminds Joseph of the nature of God: "The God who has fed me all my life long to this day, The Angel who has redeemed me from all evil" (Genesis 48:15b–16a). It is these truths that Jacob chooses to pass on. Then he says to Joseph, "Behold, I am dying, but God will be with you and bring you back to the land of your fathers" (Genesis 48:21).

Later, when it is Joseph's turn to go to be with his Lord, he says the same thing to his children. Joseph is so sure of God's promise that he gives instructions for his bones to be carried out of Egypt with them when they go to the Promised Land. Joseph's faith never wavered, not even at the end.

And so we learn our lesson. No person, no situation, no marriage, nothing at all is beyond redemption. God will not only save you, but He will use you, and make your life into something beautiful.

> Something beautiful, something good,
> All my confusion, He understood.
> All I had to offer Him
> Was brokenness and strife

But He made something
Beautiful out of my life.[2]

Nor is anybody too old to put their trust in Christ or to be used by Him. Are you eighty years old and don't know Christ as your Lord and Savior? You can know Him, if you turn to Him. Do it right now. He still wants you to reach out to Him, and He will save you.

Don't think that having a free bus pass means you can opt out of the battle either. You will have all eternity to retire in. God needs you right now. Do you know why you can have your greatest moments of faith even as an old man or woman? Because having a powerful ministry is not confined to those who are physically active. God has said:

> "Not by might nor by power, but by My Spirit," says the Lord of hosts. (Zechariah 4:6)

Whatever your age or family circumstances, invite the Spirit of the Lord of hosts to come in right now and minister healing and restoration. Then rise up in His strength and do great exploits.

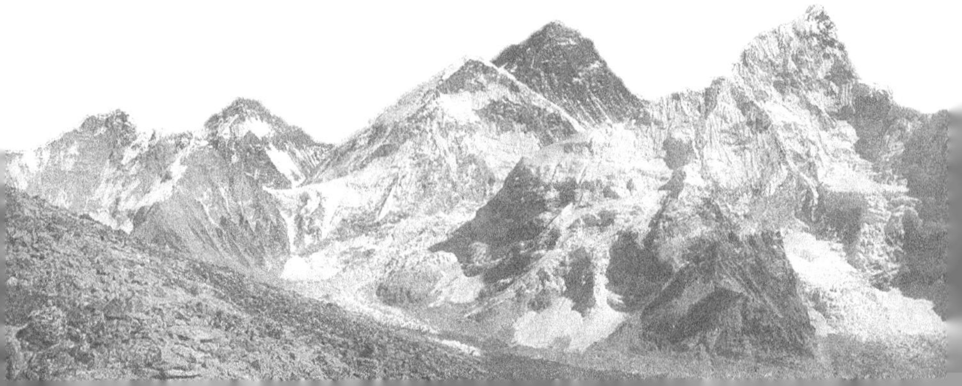

Chapter 8
THE FAITH OF THE LEADER

By faith Moses, when he was born, was hidden three months by his parents, because they saw he was a beautiful child; and they were not afraid of the king's command.

Hebrews 11:23

MORE THAN WE ASK OR THINK

GOD HAS A SENSE OF HUMOR, DON'T YOU THINK? Moses was the first baby to receive child benefit, and God brought it about in the most humorous way.

First, the baby Moses is placed in the ugliest "Moses basket" that ever existed—bulrushes daubed with asphalt and pitch! You wouldn't sell many of those in the local craft shop. Then he is discovered by Pharaoh's daughter, who decides to adopt him. However, she's not too keen on changing diapers, so she sends her maid off to hire a nanny from among the Hebrew women. Now the maid comes back with Moses' real mother. Pharaoh's daughter asks the real mother to look after the child and agrees to pay her for it. Moses' mum had faith, and God honored it in a marvelous way. She thought that she would never see Moses again, but that at least he would be safe. At that moment, however, she must have rejoiced in the reality of Ephesians 3:20, and the God "who is able to do exceedingly abundantly above all that we ask or think, according to the power that works in us." Do you know the reality of this truth in your life? Whether you are a mother concerned about the future of your child, or whether you're a pioneer missionary out on the front line, do you really believe that He is able?

George Verwer and Dale Rhoton had a burden for world evangelism. Many years ago, they led a group of students from America on a summer mission to Mexico. The next year they crossed over to Spain. In 1957 they founded Operation Mobilization, and now they have about fifteen hundred workers (perhaps twice that in the summer months) working in every continent of the world. They also have had ships manned by volunteer believers from over twenty-five countries, and all are committed to world evangelism.[1] During all of this time, God has provided for their needs. We truly have an amazing God, who wants to do more than we can ask or think!

A Wise Choice

> By faith Moses, when he became of age, refused to be called the son of Pharaoh's daughter, choosing rather to suffer affliction with the people of God than to enjoy the passing pleasures of sin, esteeming the reproach of Christ greater riches than the treasures in Egypt; for he looked to the reward. By faith he forsook Egypt, not fearing the wrath of the king; for he endured as seeing Him who is invisible. (Heb. 11:24–27)

How often, when faced with choices, do we make the wrong one? Egypt was the cultural and economic center of the world, and a great future lay before Moses. He could have had it all, but he chose another way. By faith he went God's way. Sometimes the choices we have to make are not so clear-cut as to be between good and evil. Sometimes they are between what is good and what is God's best.

The name of Billy Graham had risen to a place of prominence in America by the 1950s, and so the inevitable invitations started coming his way. A career in politics or television could have been his for the taking, and he was invited to run as senator for his own state. He declined. At times he really struggled with these issues. Like any serious believer, he wanted to make his life count. What was the best way to do that? Was it to be an evangelist, or should he aim to be President of the United States? One day, while he was deep in thought about all this, he wandered on a mountainside and started singing an old hymn:

> Rescue the perishing, care for the dying,
> Snatch them in pity from sin and the grave;
> Weep o'er the erring one, lift up the fallen,
> Tell them of Jesus, the mighty to save.

He knew without a shadow of a doubt that henceforth he must have "no other desire, no other goal, no other ambition."[2]

Moses chose to suffer affliction with the people of God rather than enjoy the passing pleasure of sin. There is no doubt that sin can be very pleasurable, but it's a pleasure that doesn't last. So we need to sin again, and before long we find that sin becomes a way of life that destroys us. Moses was a man who could see the future. By that I don't mean he had a crystal ball, but that he knew where the pathway of sin would lead him. We are told that he "esteemed the reproach of Christ greater riches than the treasures of Egypt; for he looked to the reward." Christ hadn't yet been born, but Moses knew; he looked forward; his eyes were looking to that eternal reward. These are the men and women that God can use; those with spiritual insight and the eyes of faith.

What it comes down to in the end is, how real is our God? You see, Moses lived in Egypt. He could see and touch Pharaoh, whereas God was invisible. Yet we are told that "By faith he forsook Egypt, not fearing the wrath of the king; for he endured as seeing Him who is invisible." Moses could see God. God is only invisible to the human eye, but not to the eye of faith. You and I can see God, too!

We see Him at work in people's lives; we see Him snatching sinners from the very gates of hell and turning their lives around. Look and see the glory of the King; sense the presence of the Lord among His people. Jesus is alive! There's really only one choice to make when we know God. Let's make it, and stick with it.

The Blood of the Lamb

> By faith he kept the Passover and the sprinkling of blood, lest he who destroyed the firstborn should touch them. (Hebrews 11:28)

In Exodus chapter 12 we have the gospel of Jesus Christ. The children of Israel understood the principle that sin required judgment and the shedding of blood. For their sins, they deserved to die. The only way they could live was if something died in their place—a sacrificial lamb.

Moses was still in Egypt when he instituted the Passover and the Feast of Unleavened Bread, and it was while we were still lost in our sins that Christ died for us, the ungodly.

Moses was told to take a "lamb [. . .] without blemish, a male" (Exodus 12:5). This is so significant. In the New Testament Peter says, "knowing that you were not redeemed with corruptible things, like silver or gold, from your aimless conduct received by tradition from your fathers, but with the precious blood of Christ, as of a lamb without blemish and without spot" (1 Pet. 1:18–19). Jesus was our sacrificial lamb. He took our place so that we might live.

> Surely He has borne our griefs
> And carried our sorrows;
> Yet we esteemed Him stricken,
> Smitten by God, and afflicted.
> But He was wounded for our transgressions,
> He was bruised for our iniquities
> The chastisement for our peace was upon Him,
> And by His stripes we are healed.

> All we like sheep have gone astray
> We have turned, every one, to his own way;
> And the Lord has laid on Him
> The iniquity of us all.
> He was oppressed and He was afflicted,
> Yet He opened not His mouth;
> He was led as a lamb to the slaughter.
> (Isaiah 53:4–7)

Jesus made atonement for our sins. He became the ultimate scapegoat (Leviticus 16:20–22). Did Moses understand the significance of this? We do not know; but we know that he had faith in God.

At that first Passover, God told Moses to dip hyssop into the blood of the lamb and smear it on the doorposts. That night God would pass through to strike the Egyptians, but would pass over the doorposts that had the blood. By faith this is what they did, and they lived.

On the final day of judgment, if we want God to "pass over" us and not throw us into the lake of fire, just as God needed to see the blood then, He needs to see it now. He needs to see that we have put our faith in the blood of the Lamb. Jesus is the perfect Lamb; the Lamb that is worthy (Revelation 5:9). Our filthy lives can be washed and made white in the blood of the Lamb (Rev. 7:14).

> And can it be that I should gain
> An interest in the Savior's blood?
> Died He for me, who caused His pain,
> For me, who Him, to death pursued.
> Amazing love, how can it be,
> That thou, my God,
> Shouldst die for me.
> (Charles Wesley, 1738)

Faith for Every Emergency

> By faith they passed through the Red Sea as by dry land, whereas the Egyptians, attempting to do so, were drowned. (Hebrews 11:29)

Hudson Taylor's voyage to China was fraught with problems. One particularly dangerous time came as they sailed close to Papua New Guinea. The wind had completely disappeared and the current was carrying the ship toward a sunken reef. It seemed inevitable that the ship would be wrecked.

The captain said that nothing could be done. Young Taylor, however, said that there was still one thing they hadn't tried. They should pray and ask God to immediately send a wind. This they did. Hudson Taylor returned to his cabin for what turned out to be a good yet brief time of prayer. He felt so satisfied that his request had been granted that he stopped beseeching and went back out on deck. He told a sailor to raise the sail because the wind was coming. The man thought he was a fool. Nevertheless, the wind came. Immediately! And it soon carried the ship to safety.

"Thus," wrote Hudson, "God encouraged me, ere landing on China's shores, to bring every variety of need to Him in prayer, and to expect that He would honor the Name of the Lord Jesus, and give the help which each emergency required."[3]

So Moses led the children of Israel out of Egypt, and they went out boldly. However, the Egyptians pursued them. God told Moses that they should camp by the sea opposite Baal Zephon but it left them trapped with nowhere to go. Soon the Egyptians were upon them, and they were hemmed in: by Pharaoh's army on one side, the Red Sea on the other.

The Israelites grumbled at their leader; not an uncommon response when things go wrong, even among God's people. Moses put on a brave face. He did all that a leader should do. With exuberant confidence he said, "Do not be afraid. Stand still, and see the salvation of the Lord, which He will accomplish for you today" (Exodus 14:13). Now that's faith! Anybody in such a situation, who can say that, has got faith. What was that faith built on? The sure knowledge that the battle was God's, not theirs. They were only God's ambassadors, His representatives, and like any ambassador, Moses knew that he could count on the full support of the One who had commissioned him and sent him out. At least, that's the theory!

It's the reality, too, but our feelings don't always line themselves up with what we know to be true. They don't for us, and they didn't for Moses.

The Lord said to Moses, "Why do you cry to Me?" (Exodus 14:15a). Obviously, while Moses was putting on a brave face before his men, he was inwardly panicking and crying out, "Help!" Fortunately, we don't need to worry too much about those feelings; God's Word will hold true no matter how we feel. But our testimony is stronger when the feelings fall into line. I believe God will meet my financial needs, but that is no testimony at all if I become a nervous wreck in the process! It is inevitable, though, that we will have times of doubt when so much is at stake. On the whole, Moses is a tremendous example of leadership.

So God said to Moses, "Tell the children of Israel to go forward. But lift up your rod, and stretch out your hand over the sea and divide it" (Ex. 14:15b–16a). Notice here that God doesn't say, "Ask Me to divide it." No, the command is for Moses to divide the sea. Sometimes God wants His people to exercise authority in His name. It doesn't mean that we should get all puffed up and act like gods ourselves; we can do nothing without Him. However, if we are Christians, He lives in us. Jesus told His disciples that all authority had been given to Him, and that He would be with them until the end of the age. Sometimes I think God wants us to stop asking Him to do everything and to get on with the job.

God did two amazing miracles here. First, He made it completely dark where the Egyptians were, while at the same time, just down the road, it was light for the Israelites so that they could see. Then God parted the waters of the Red Sea.

This wasn't an instant miracle. We love instant miracles, don't we? And they are an encouragement to us. But true faith is often formed through time and testing; like the person who perhaps prays fifty years for that unsaved relative to come to Christ—always hoping, always believing, prevailing in prayer.

We are told that Moses held out his arm over the sea, and God caused the waters to part. A strong east wind that blew all night caused the seas to pile up, and the children of Israel walked across on dry land. It had been an emergency situation. Moses trusted his God, and God saw him through.

When the Egyptians tried to follow, God told Moses to stretch out his hand over the sea again to bring the waters back down on the Egyptians. I find it interesting that once again God told Moses to do it. He didn't bypass Moses and do it Himself. I wonder why? I think perhaps He was teaching an important principle here. Moses was the leader, and God didn't want to undermine him before the Israelites. Of course, we know that God was the ultimate leader, but, nevertheless, He had established Moses, and He wanted to build him up in front of the people, not knock him down. God knew how to delegate. He didn't just pass on responsibility; He gave the authority to go with it and stood by the man He chose.

We all know what happened next. The Egyptians were drowned as the walls of water came breaking down over them. Some cynics have tried to say that Moses and the Israelites didn't cross the Red Sea, rather it was the Reed Sea, which is just a marsh with no more than two feet of water. Whenever anyone opens their mouth to criticize the Bible, they always put their foot in it, don't they? I mean, can you imagine the entire Egyptian army drowning in two feet of water?

Chapter 9
WHERE THE ACTION IS

By faith the walls of Jericho fell down after they were encircled for seven days. By faith the harlot Rahab did not perish with those who did not believe, when she had received the spies with peace.

And what more shall I say? For the time would fail me to tell of Gideon and Barak and Samson and Jephthah, also of David and Samuel and the prophets: who through faith subdued kingdoms, worked righteousness, obtained promises, stopped the mouths of lions, quenched the violence of fire, escaped the edge of the sword, out of weakness were made strong, became valiant in battle, turned to flight the armies of the aliens.

Hebrews 11:30–34

I WAS IN THE PULPIT OF A SMALL, INNER-CITY church in London, England, and had just given the call to worship when the most amazing thing happened. But before I tell you about that, let me explain how I came to be there in the first place.

For three years I had not had a single preaching engagement, and I didn't understand why. I knew that the Lord had called me to preach. I had already preached in Southeast Asia, both in churches and in the open air. Now back in Britain, all had come to a standstill. I still held to my policy of not pushing myself forward for or soliciting speaking engagements. I had seen the way that some people did that and had found it appalling. If I were to preach, God would work it out. But He hadn't, and so I asked Him "Why?" I got an answer very quickly, and I knew what the Lord was saying to me. He was saying, "If you want to preach, then preach; every street corner can be your pulpit." It made sense, of course. Jesus wasn't always in great demand as a speaker. More often than not you would find Him out on the streets where the action was. I resolved to do the same—so I started preaching on the streets. Not just preaching, but doing all kinds of street evangelism. Although nobody knew of my decision, it happened almost simultaneously that preaching opportunities from churches started to come, and my preaching ministry grew from there.

Shortly after that I met Trevor Florey, a man whose ministry involves finding preachers for churches with no pastor. Many of these churches were in the inner city, and he wanted me to be one of his preachers. I was glad to be. I lived in the inner city, and it was there that God was using me the most. However, before Trevor was going to let me loose in these churches, he wanted to check me out. So he came with me on my first engagement. I was quite nervous at the thought of my preaching being assessed.

So there I was, and as I said, I had just given the call to worship when an incredible thing happened. The door of the church burst open with a huge crash. Every head in the congregation turned and saw a young man stagger up the aisle. I knew that he was high on drugs. He was also covered with patches of blood, and he started swearing and cursing.

"I've just been in a knife fight. They're after me and will get me tonight. I don't know if I'm coming or going. I don't believe in God, but I'm desperate. If there is anything in this God stuff, I want to know, and I want to know now!"

"Er, yes, my friend," I mumbled, "please come in and sit down." He had already done both! My heart raced. As an evangelist I was glad of this opportunity. As a stand-in pastor being assessed on my ability to conduct a service, I thought, *Oh no, I don't believe it.*

"Brothers and sisters, I do believe that God is telling us not to worry if we don't stick to our original order of service today." I needn't have worried, for as I looked around (I didn't look at Trevor!) I could see that everyone was right behind me. They were real saints. In each face I saw the message, "Go ahead—don't worry about us!"

So I continued, and drew on everything I knew to present the gospel to our friend from the streets. At times I knew I was getting through. I could see that he was under conviction. At other times it looked as if I had lost him, and he would let out a curse. Sometimes his curses were blasphemous. What was I to do? I was in charge, and he was blaspheming in the house of God. What was Trevor thinking? I decided that this man's soul was more important than anything else, and I kept going. Soon he was on his feet and moving toward the back of the church.

"Trevor, please take over," I pleaded, and I followed the young man out. We stood outside talking, while those inside the church prayed. I gave him some literature and prayed with him. I just couldn't tell how much was getting through, as he was out of his mind on drugs. Then suddenly he ran away. I chased after him. We were running through narrow alleyways and jumping over fences, but he knew his way around better than I did, and I lost him. I wandered back to the church. I was sweaty and dirty, and my suit was in a mess. I thought about Trevor, and said to myself, "I wonder if I've passed?"

Not all my speaking engagements since then have been quite like that one. However, I have learned one thing—that God is desperately looking for people to be out on the front line. He loves those people whose lives are all messed up, and He only has you and me to use as channels of forgiveness, healing, and restoration. We are always praying in our churches to be blessed, but I believe that God has a special blessing for those who will roll up their sleeves and get their hands dirty. If you want blessing, get where the action is, for there you will find God in a special way. Let's look at some of God's men of action.

Joshua and the Victory of Faith

In a letter to a certain Miss Chalmers, Scotland's national poet Robbie Burns wrote:

> I have taken tooth and nail to the Bible, and am got through the five books of Moses, and half-way in Joshua. It is really a glorious book.[1]

It is indeed a glorious book. Whether Burns was referring to the book of Joshua or to the whole Bible is not certain, but in both cases he was right. And Joshua is a glorious character, for in him we can see and understand what is meant by "the victory of faith."

One of the first things we should notice about Joshua is that he was a faithful servant. For eighty years Joshua ministered behind the scenes. He was the original unsung hero, content to serve and support Moses. Loyalty to another person is no longer as common place as it used to be, and the church is much the worse for it. Joshua was content to serve another. Later on we see David showing intense loyalty to Saul, even though Saul was out to kill him. David acknowledged that Saul had been put in his position by God (1 Samuel 24:6). Today we say that "respect needs to be earned," and of course there is truth in that, but it is not the whole picture. Are children free to disobey parents and teachers just because they haven't earned their respect? Should the crew of a ship disobey the captain, or the navigator of an airplane disobey the pilot simply because they don't respect him as a person? If this were to happen, tragedy would quickly follow, and yet sadly we find this state of affairs all too often in the church. Rebellion against God's anointed because they don't shape up to our expectations is never right. Joshua was loyal; he was faithful in the little things, and so God entrusted him with greater things.

After Moses' death, God commissioned Joshua: "Be strong and of good courage, do not be afraid, nor be dismayed, for the Lord your God is with you wherever you go" (Joshua 1:9). What a promise from God to Joshua! God repeatedly tells Joshua to be strong. From this we perhaps learn that Joshua, without God's help, was not your typical strong man. God wants His people to be bold and strong, but only as they recognize their own weakness, apart from Him, can that be possible (2 Corinthians 12:9). Joshua could go forward in the strength of God Himself—and he did.

It has become popular in recent years to teach that you no longer need a "call" into ministry. It is said, rather, that we are all called to evangelize the world, the Great Commission being our call. Now I know what is meant here, and I would go along with it, to a point. However, I believe firmly that God has specific tasks for people to do. Ephesians 2:10 says:

> For we are His workmanship, created in Christ Jesus for good works, which God prepared beforehand that we should walk in them.

It is important to make a distinction here. We do not need a call to join our church's outreach program, or to help in the office of a local mission, but we do need a call to uproot our families and go plant a church among some jungle tribe, or to launch an ambitious project that is going to affect a lot of people. For if we embark upon such a project without the assurance that we are doing God's specific will, how will we stick with it when the opposition comes? Satan will not stand idly by. The call may not be something tangible; it may just be an inner assurance or compulsion, as when Paul said, "Woe is me if I do not preach the gospel!" (1 Corinthians 9:16), but nevertheless it is important. Time after time, the kingdom of God has lost out because of a misunderstanding of these issues. People have held back because they didn't feel called, when they didn't need to; others have rushed ahead on outrageous projects without a call, when they did need one. Later on, Joshua learned this lesson the hard way.

In Jericho's Red Light Area

The promises that were given to Moses were passed on to Joshua. So, in preparation for possessing the land, Joshua sent two spies ahead to check out the city of Jericho while the others prepared for the three-day journey.

The two spies ended up lodging at the home of a prostitute, Rahab. What happens next is enough to secure even Rahab the prostitute a place in the Heroes' Hall of Fame that is Hebrews 11. Is this a mistake? Or is there an important lesson to learn here?

When the king of Jericho heard what was going on, he sent his men to Rahab's house to capture the spies. However, Rahab had hidden them on the roof and then lied to the king's men, saying that they had already left. Is it ever permissible for a Christian to lie? I think the answer is yes. A higher ethic is involved here. Imagine if this had been two British soldiers during the Second World War, and they had taken refuge in the farmhouse of a Christian lady in occupied France, and the Nazis came searching for them. Would the Christian thing to do be to hand them over to the Nazis? No. So I think Rahab was right to lie. However, we cannot be sure. Hebrews 11 remembers her for her faith, not her lie! Perhaps she should have had the faith to trust God to enable her to deal with the problem without lying.

When the incident was over, Rahab returned to the hidden men and said:

> "I know that the Lord has given you the land, that the terror of you has fallen on us, and that all the inhabitants of the land are fainthearted because of you." (Joshua 2:9)

This confirms what we were looking at in Chapter 1—that the power of God's presence is more terrifying than the knife blade, or even a mighty army. Rahab feared the Lord! The Lord's reputation had preceded Him, and Rahab believed. God is no respecter of persons. In Romans 10:13 we are told that whoever calls on the name of the Lord shall be saved. This is, in effect, what Rahab did when, privately in her heart and publicly with her lips, she acknowledged the truth of who God is by saying:

> The Lord your God, He is God in heaven above and on earth beneath. (Joshua 2:11)

Salvation had come to Rahab, who had to live and make choices in difficult circumstances. So, whoever you are, and whatever situation you find yourself in, this same salvation can be yours too.

Are You Standing in the Jordan?

So the spies returned, and the Israelites continued their journey. God had promised Joshua that He would be with him in the same way as He had been with Moses. To demonstrate this, God intended to part the waters of the Jordan just like He had done with the Red Sea. God, therefore, gave instructions to Joshua that he was to send the priests who were carrying the Ark of the Covenant down to the banks of the river, and to tell them to step into the water. It was very important that they stepped in it.

I have found time and time again that here is an important principle of faith. We must make the first move. Jesus didn't turn the sea into concrete so that Peter could step out of the boat and onto the water. No, Peter had to step out onto the water and the water supported him. Perhaps you're in a position of leadership that you feel you should resign from, but you can't find a replacement. Maybe you should resign anyway and leave that to God. Or you know that God wants you to embark on a project, but rather than begin, you're waiting for Him to make all the details clear first. Maybe you are trusting God for money for a particular initiative, but have you opened a bank account yet, so that you can receive funds? Can you win a person to Christ without first speaking to him? Can the rudder of a ship have any impact on the direction of sail unless the ship is moving? The principle is simply this: we must walk by faith and not by sight.

So, you're standing in the water holding the Ark of the Covenant, and one of your old workmates comes by.

"Hey, what're you doing, Charlie?"

"Oh, I'm just waiting for God to part the waters so we can walk across the river."

You see, faith that isn't on the line isn't faith at all.

But the waters of the Jordan were heaped up, and the Israelites crossed over, just as their fathers had crossed the Red Sea before them. Then God told them to erect a monument with twelve stones, representing the twelve tribes of Israel, at Gilgal, where they camped that night. How important it is that we should remember the things that God has done for us.

And so they came to Jericho, which had been secured in anticipation of their arrival.

> And the Lord said to Joshua: "See! I have given Jericho into your hand, its king, and the mighty men of valor." (Joshua 6:2)

Joshua could see no such thing, at least not with his human eyes, but he could with eyes of faith. What God said next was quite amazing:

> You shall march around the city, all you men of war; you shall go all around the city once. This you shall do six days. And seven priests shall bear the seven trumpets of ram's horns before the ark. But the seventh day you shall march around the city seven times, and the priests shall blow the trumpets. It shall come to pass, when they make a long blast with the ram's horn, and when you hear the sound of the trumpet, that all the people shall shout with a great shout; then the wall of the city will fall down flat. And the people shall go up every man straight before him. (Joshua 6:3–5)

What was all this? Full-grown men, soldiers at that, playing ring a ring o' roses! Now Joshua's faith really was on the line. Imagine if you were the commander of a battalion of troops, and you gave them orders like that. Wouldn't you feel stupid? Of course you would; so would I. Anybody would. But Joshua was willing to be a fool for Christ. He didn't mind sticking his neck out or going out on a limb for His Lord. He knew that God wouldn't saw the limb off once he was out there!

So he gave instructions, and the men started marching round. We cannot put into print the language they must have used among themselves at that moment! When they had agreed to follow Joshua, they hadn't realized he was unbalanced. Nevertheless, they did as they were told.

All the time this was going on, Joshua was a shining example of confidence. On the inside, however, he must have been stewing; at least when the moment came to shout. I can just imagine a sick look on his face.

"Well, here goes. Let's hope that it's the walls that are destroyed, and not my reputation."

The moment came, the priests blew their trumpets, and Joshua cried:

> "Shout, for the Lord has given you the city!"
> (Joshua 6:16)

And lo, the wall fell down flat. The victory of faith (that's faith on the line) had been secured.

Joshua and the Failure of Presumption

While it is not in our Hebrews 11 text, I think that it is appropriate, before moving on to our next heroes of faith, to consider what, for Joshua, came after Jericho. As so often happens after a great victory, we easily fail and fall into defeat. The sin of presumption quickly sets in, and before we know it we have fallen flat on our faces.

The next city to be conquered was Ai. Again Joshua sent spies to check the place out. On their return they boasted, "Do not let all the people go up, but let about two or three thousand men go up and attack Ai. Do not weary all the people there, for the people of Ai are few" (Joshua 7:3). Their victory at Jericho had gone to their heads. Not only that, but Joshua's men disobeyed him by looting and plundering Jericho when he had told them not to. Needless to say, the mission to Ai was a disaster. The three thousand men of Joshua's army had to flee for their lives.

Some years ago my wife Hilary, and I, and a friend started a Christian community in southeast London. From the start we saw the hand of God upon the project, even though it was fraught with problems and difficulties. We took in refugees from Vietnam and sought to live a New Testament lifestyle. We were very naive, and I wouldn't pretend for one moment that this was "heaven on earth." Nevertheless, God was with us. It wasn't long before we were planning to open a second such house in Birmingham, in England's West Midlands. Somebody there indicated that they would like to sell their house and get a bigger one to use for this purpose. We were moving ahead with our plans, and I emphasize the word "our," because we hadn't included God in this project very much. We announced our intentions in our newsletter so that all those who supported us could pray. But we got it wrong. The London house was of the Spirit, but the Birmingham house was of the flesh. We had to humble ourselves and admit that we had crossed the barrier from faith to presumption. It is so easy to do.

What it all comes down to in the end is walking with God. We have to be walking in the Spirit, yielding our lives to His direction, instead of insisting that He put a stamp of approval on our ideas. I had to wrestle with this very same issue over our Seacare project. It is quite a responsibility to step out and trust God for a ship. Were we really moving in faith, or were we being presumptuous? It is not always easy to know. For five years I wrestled with this dilemma before making our intentions known to others. One of the ways God sometimes makes His will known to me is by putting me in a position where, having explored all the alternatives, there is only one way that I can go that gives me an inner peace and assurance. As soon as I try to go in any other direction, that assurance disappears.

Of course it is important to follow all the other parameters for guidance, too; such as being submitted to the leadership of a local church, getting the advice of mature believers, and being in prayer and in God's Word. The only way we can be sure we are moving in faith and not presumption is for the branches—that's us—to remain firmly connected to the Vine, which is Jesus (John 15:1–8). It is better to walk in the Spirit than to learn the hard way!

And What More Shall I Say?

Is there time to tell of Gideon, Barak, Samson, Jephthah, David, Samuel and the prophets? The writer to the Hebrews thought not. To do each of these characters justice would mean writing several books, not just one. However, let us at least pick out one or two principles that will help us in our adventure in faith.

Gideon (Judges 6–8)
Principle: God works through our personality, He doesn't bypass it.

> And the Angel of the Lord appeared to him, and said to him, "The Lord is with you, you mighty man of valor!" (Judges 6:12).

Does that sound strange? Can God be impressed by our mighty valor? We are not at all accustomed to thinking like this, are we? Such a person as this would surely need to be broken before God could use him. However, what does God say to Gideon?

> "Go in this might of yours, and you shall save Israel from the hand of the Midianites. Have I not sent you?" (Judges 6:14)

"Go in this might of yours"? What is God saying here?

I think we misunderstand the concept of humility sometimes. I remember once giving a financial gift to a missionary who obviously had some problems receiving it. "Oh, thanks for your obedience," he said. I walked away wondering if he really believed that God had told me to give him the money but that I myself hadn't wanted to; nevertheless, I was obedient! I don't think God works like that, do you? Certainly, it was a gift from God, but He had inspired me to want to give it. I'm not a robot; I'm a person. He can bypass our personhood if He wants to, but that's not His usual way.

It is the same with those people who can't receive a compliment. "Oh, don't thank me, it was the Lord." I don't believe God wants us to be like that. I think He wants us to graciously receive those compliments. We know it was the Lord; that's what matters. And later on, we can perhaps witness to that fact.

I think the lesson God was teaching Gideon here is that he would indeed become a mighty man of valor, but that would be because God was with him. God wasn't going to dehumanize Gideon and make him into a robot just to accomplish His purposes. No: God intended to make Gideon into the kind of person he was always meant to be—bold, strong and valiant. This, as Christians, is what our testimony should be. Instead of saying, "It wasn't me, it was Christ," we can confidently say, "It was me, the new me, but it's *because* of Christ." Now that is a powerful testimony. Gideon went into battle with these words, "The sword of the Lord and of Gideon!" (Judges 7:18) Think about it.

Barak (Judges 4–5)
Principle: A vision of the Church.
Judges chapter 5 is the song that Deborah and Barak sang on the day of their victory over the king of Canaan. It starts out with these words:

> "When leaders lead in Israel,
> When the people willingly offer themselves,
> Bless the Lord!"
> (Judges 5:2)

Now if ever there was a vision, a blueprint for the Church, that is it. Imagine a church where the leaders lead and the congregation willingly offer themselves. And Deborah and Barak practiced what they preached; Barak had just led the Israelites to great victory, and Deborah had willingly accompanied Barak when he requested her to do so.

The song finishes with these words:

> "But let those who love Him be like the sun
> when it comes out in full strength."
> (Judges 5:31b)

Yes, truly a picture of how the people of God are meant to be: a dazzling light, a people on fire for God.

Samson (Judges 13–16)

Principle: The man or woman God uses may not be our choice.

I feel for Samson. Traditional evangelical teaching has not been kind to him. We are told that he was immoral, foolish, presumptuous and all manner of other things—and he was! There is no denying the truth of that. However, in Hebrews 11 he is not remembered for any of those traits, but rather as a man of faith.

C. S. Lewis once said that he was "amazed at the man God uses." You see that we may sometimes get things wrong. But there must have been something there, in the beginning at least, in Samson that God saw. Let me itemize some of the good things about Samson that can be found in Judges 13 to 16.

1. He was more concerned about the kingdom of God than anyone else in his generation.
2. His personal failures were not as great as those of David or Solomon.
3. The Spirit of God came upon him mightily.
4. He understood that his ministry was given to him by God.
5. He embraced the Nazarite vow, clearly nailing his colors to the mast.

6. He abided in his calling.
7. He exercised faith.
8. He was concerned about justice.
9. He "went it alone" when others were not interested.
10. He provoked the enemy to retaliate. (Does our ministry do the same?)

I will stop there, though we have not exhausted Samson's good points by any means. I do not want to make light of his failings, but I for one can see why he is mentioned in Hebrews 11. He may not have been our choice, but God saw things that evangelical tradition has missed.[2]

Jephthah (Judges 11–12)
Principle: Don't call unclean what the Lord has called clean.
Some friends of mine were visiting a church in the Southern States. They had left their children in the nursery. The youngest one, however, would not settle, and so the mother said to the lady in charge, "If you want to go and hear the sermon, go ahead. I've got to stay here anyway." "I can't," replied the woman, "they won't allow black people in the church." The year was not 1897, but 1987! It's hard to believe attitudes like that still exist today, but even now in 2020 they do in some places.

Jephthah was a mighty man of valor, but that wasn't enough to gain acceptance among the religious people of his day. You see, he was the son of a prostitute. We love to hear the testimonies of people who have been converted from a terrible background, but we are not always so keen when they want to join our church. At least, that's what it's like in some churches. Jephthah became an outcast, not just from the church, but from the whole nation. However, things did not go too well for the nation, and they realized that they needed Jephthah. People can be very fickle. So they asked him to come back and lead them into battle against the Ammonites. Jephthah agreed. The Spirit of God came upon him and gave him victory.

God once gave a vision to Peter (Acts 10:9–16) to impress upon him that he must not call unclean that which God has made clean. It is an important lesson that we need to learn.

Normally, our mission – Christian Care Projects, and our ship project, Seacare – does not accept people who are not committed to a local church. It is usually a sign that something is wrong when God's people don't want to fellowship together. However, we do occasionally come across someone who desperately wants to be committed to a church, but can't find one that will be committed to them. This is not so much the case in big cities, but in some rural areas and in a number of other countries it is quite common. In such cases as these, perhaps when the person has been involved in drugs and the occult, or worse, we will still take them on. After all, Jesus did! Our first priority would be to find them a church, because a parachurch organization should never take over the role of the church. Together with the church, we will disciple them; but it's a give and take relationship. Such people have a lot to give, too. Those who have been forgiven much are often those who love much (Luke 7:47). And like Jephthah, they can become great leaders.

Samuel (1 Samuel 1–3)
Principle: Children are a gift from God, and should be a gift to God. We should never take children for granted. Hannah couldn't, because she was unable to have any herself, and it made her miserable. However, she petitioned God in prayer and came to a place of peace. Now she was no longer miserable, but she worshiped God. And lo and behold, it came to pass that God gave Hannah a son, and she called him Samuel, which means "heard by God."

Hannah did not forget about her prayer. She was determined to credit God with this miracle child. After she had weaned Samuel, she dedicated him to God. The act of dedicating a child to God should never be just a one-off ceremony; rather it should represent a continuing attitude of releasing the child to God. It is so easy to become possessive and overprotective, but God has plans for our children, far greater than we ever could have.

"But Samuel ministered before the Lord, even as a child" (1 Samuel 2:18). Is it possible for children to have a ministry? Of course, especially if the adults are not responding in obedience to God's Word. 1 Samuel 3:1 says, "Now the boy Samuel ministered to the Lord before Eli. And the word of the Lord was rare in those days; there was no widespread revelation."

Many years ago my own fellowship then, St. Mildred's in southeast London, England, had been a typical Anglican church full of "good people." Then somebody visited St. Mildred's who had not been a regular attender (though many had prayed that He would soon make a visit). His name—the Holy Spirit! Yes, the Spirit of God swept through the church, bringing renewal and life. And it was largely the prayers of the young people that brought it about. Young people have a lot to learn. Yes, they need to be discipled. But they also have a lot to offer, in the hands of our living God.

David (1 Samuel 16–2 Samuel 24)

Principle: A man or woman after God's heart.

"He's always messing up, but his heart's in the right place." A familiar testimony, and one which is very applicable to David. To be fair, David didn't really mess up that often, but when he did, he certainly did it properly.

There are two mistakes that David made which really stand out. The one he's best known for is the Bathsheba incident (2 Samuel 11), which involved David in adultery that led to murder. However, only three people died in that case, compared to seventy thousand who lost their lives in the second incident, when David started trusting in himself and his own resources instead of in his great God (2 Samuel 24).

Despite all this, though, God loved him; because, as we are told, he was "a man after God's own heart" (1 Samuel 13:14). Notice what his motivation was when, as a young lad, he took on the giant, Goliath. He took on Goliath because, as he said, "he has defied the armies of the living God" (1 Samuel 17:36). David's faith did not waver; he knew that his God was with him. Confidently, he said to Goliath, "You come to me with a sword, with a spear, and with a javelin. But I come to you in the name of the Lord of hosts . . ." (1 Samuel 17:45) And in the next verse David told Goliath that God would deliver him into his hand; "that all the earth may know that there is a God in Israel." You see, what mattered to David was God's reputation. It was God's honor that was the motivating force in his life, and it should be in ours, too.

In David we see a man who really had a tremendous relationship with God: he esteemed God so much. Of course God was not pleased with David's sin, but what is more important to any parent, that their children never make any mistakes, or that their children love them?

In 2 Samuel 24:24 David makes a statement which has had a great impact on my life. He planned to make an offering to the Lord and wanted to buy the threshing floor and the oxen from Araunah, their owner, but Araunah wanted to give them to David. David would not hear of it:

> "nor will I offer burnt offerings to the Lord my God with that which costs me nothing."

Are we seeking to offer to God that which costs us nothing? Can God say of us that we are men and women after his own heart?

> For the eyes of the Lord run to and fro throughout the whole earth, to show Himself strong on behalf of those whose heart is loyal to Him. (2 Chronicles 16:9)

Those who are loyal, not those who are perfect. No, ordinary people: young or old, black or white, brought up in Christian homes or the children of parents living an unhelpful lifestyle. God is no respecter of persons. Trust Him. Don't be afraid to get where the action is.

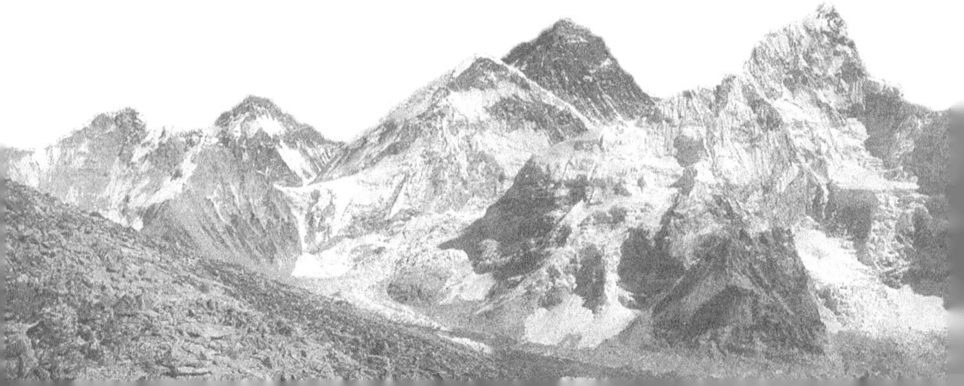

Chapter 10
RAISING THE DEAD

Women received their dead raised to life again.

Hebrews 11:35a

THE NISHA TRIBES IN THE SULANSINI DIVISION of northeast India are now receptive to the miraculous. It all started when the youngest son of a high-up government official fell terminally ill.

A Hindu pharmacist, recognizing that the child was beyond medical help, advised the father, "Try the Christian God, Jesus Christ. I have heard that He raised a man called Lazarus who had already been dead for three days!" As the father approached his house, he heard crying and wailing, and he knew that his son must have died. He went into the house and discovered that it was so. But then he went into the son's room, placed his hand on the chest of his dead son and prayed, "Jesus, I do not know who you are, but I have heard that you raised Lazarus from the dead after three days. My son has died only a few hours ago, and if you raise him up, I promise you, even though I do not know who you are, my family and I will worship you." Immediately the eyes of the child began to flicker again, and he was restored to life. The impact of the miracle was tremendous. The people cried, "Jesus, who are you? What love you have for us!" Within the next couple of weeks, hundreds gave their lives to Jesus.[1]

The Theology

There are those who suppose that miracles, signs and wonders, tongues, and prophecy (in fact, just about anything supernatural) went out with the first apostles. They would argue that the signs of Pentecost were given for the Jews to see, as a warning that the kingdom was again drawing near, so that they could respond. When they still did not, both the kingdom and the signs were supposed to have been withdrawn.

Personally, I cannot go along with this view, though I have many friends and know many respected colleagues who do. However, we are all responsible individually for our own interpretation of Scripture. We cannot rest on another person's understanding of it. I for one (and there are many more like me) cannot come to any other conclusion than this: if anything at all went out with those early apostles, it was faith and commitment. Certainly there is no shortage of miracles in the world today when those two ingredients are mixed together. God hasn't changed, but many of His followers today bear little resemblance to those early apostles, and consequently they don't see God at work in the same way. On the other hand, the Charismatic Church has often been accused of immaturity and excess. But is that a reason to "throw the baby out with the bathwater"?

I once met a Christian leader who said that he had not heard a message on spiritual gifts in seventeen years! Are we any better than those who go a little overboard if we are not teaching the full counsel of God? I for one do not want to be a "pendulum Christian," constantly overreacting to every excess I hear about. I believe that it is possible to charter a course through the center of the channel. I do not want to be labeled, for I am not one thing or the other. I am just a simple fellow who takes God at His word. You can be the same—"enjoy the wheat and spit out the straw." The people who know their God do not need to be surrounded by those who think exactly as they do. No, they are much more secure than that. They can fellowship not only with others who have different views about these secondary issues, but they can even esteem them as "better than himself" (Philippians 2:3).

Before I offer my reasons for believing that all the gifts of the Spirit, the working of miracles, and yes even occasionally, the raising of the dead (I explain later why this is the exception not the rule) are for today; let us take a look at the prophecy of Joel, which some people use to support the opposing view. You may recall that Peter quoted it on the day of Pentecost:

> "And it shall come to pass in the last days," says God,
> "that I will pour out of My Spirit on all flesh;
> your sons and your daughters shall prophesy,
> your young men shall see visions,
> your old men shall dream dreams.
> And on My menservants and on My maidservants
> I will pour out My Spirit in those days;
> and they shall prophesy.
> "I will show wonders in heaven above
> and signs in the earth beneath:
> blood and fire and vapor of smoke.
> The sun shall be turned into darkness,
> and the moon into blood,
> before the coming of the great and awesome day
> of the Lord.
> And it shall come to pass
> that whoever calls on the name of the Lord
> shall be saved."
> (Acts 2:17–21, from Joel 2:28–32a)

Was the prophecy of Joel fulfilled at Pentecost? There are some who answer yes, and then say that the signs were later withdrawn. Others say that this prophecy has not yet been fulfilled at all, and will only be fulfilled when Christ returns. Then there are those, myself included, who would say that the prophecy was fulfilled in part at Pentecost and will be fulfilled in full at the second coming. I believe, therefore, that tongues, prophecy, miracles, and so on, are for the church between these two dates. I offer the following reasons for my conclusion:

1. If the events at Pentecost were not at least part of what Joel prophesied, why did Peter say that they were (Acts 2:16)?
2. If a basic principle of Bible interpretation is "to use Scripture to interpret Scripture," then which Scripture verse or passage tells us that the signs were withdrawn?
3. If these signs were withdrawn at that time, then all the great men and women of God throughout church history, who have been mightily used in this way, were really nothing more than professional con men or tragically deluded individuals.
4. When Jesus gave His disciples the great commission to evangelize the world (Mark 16:14–20), He told them that "these signs will follow those who believe . . ." and He went on to talk about casting out demons, speaking in tongues, taking up serpents, drinking poisons without suffering any harmful effects, and healing the sick. We are then told that the disciples went out and did just this. Jesus did not say that the signs would follow only for a while.

Before we dismiss these words of Jesus because they are not in the other gospels, remember that 2 Timothy 3:16 states that all Scripture is God-breathed.

5. The prophecy could not have been fulfilled completely at Pentecost because the moon did not turn into blood. That is clearly a reference to the second coming of Christ as explained in Revelation 6:12.

Now we should point out, to be strictly accurate, that Joel's prophecy does not talk so much about miracles as about prophecy, visions and speaking in tongues. Signs and wonders are nothing new, nor did they just arrive on the scene at Pentecost. The Old Testament is a catalogue of God at work in this way. However, Peter saw fit to quote this particular prophecy at Pentecost. This was the start of a new age, the Church age, in which believers could expect to begin functioning as a body, exercising spiritual gifts.

We are exhorted in 1 Corinthians 12:1 not to be ignorant about spiritual gifts. It's ironic that this is perhaps the one area of Scripture about which we *are* the most ignorant. Nine distinct gifts are mentioned in this chapter, and they fall into three groups, as follows:

UTTERANCE	POWER	REVELATION
Prophecy	Faith	Word of knowledge
Tongues	Healing	Word of wisdom
Interpretation of tongues	Miracles	Discerning of spirits

If some or all of these gifts went out with the apostolic age, then why did God devote so much of Holy Scripture to them? Wouldn't it have been pointless if He had intended to withdraw them? How many millions of working hours would be wasted by His people in seeking gifts that were no longer available?

We should also ask this question—does God think we are better, more capable, than the early apostles? If the answer is no, then why would He expect us to wage war with the same enemy but with fewer weapons at our disposal?

It would be interesting to conduct a survey among new converts to find out how many of them believe that these signs and miracles are no longer available for us today. Very few, I should think, if any! It is only after they have been around for a few years in the presence of "more mature" Christians that unbelief and doubt set in. Some of us, instead of honestly admitting that we have fallen short of what God wants to do in our lives, have rewritten the Bible to fit our own experience (or rather lack of experience). God have mercy! God grant that, instead, we might become the kind of people who seek to bring our level of experience up to what God says it can be.

A Word of Warning

A word of warning would not go amiss here. In certain parts of the world I have heard it said, quite frequently by some, that the signs and wonders movement is not a work of God, but a work of Satan, and that the miracles that take place are counterfeit. While I agree that Satan can work miracles, and that we do need to be discerning, this kind of talk is foolish and very dangerous.

In Matthew 12:22–32 we read the account of Jesus casting out evil spirits from a demon-possessed mute. The Pharisees, however, are not impressed, and accuse Jesus of casting out demons in the name of Beelzebub. Jesus explains the futility of this kind of thinking: "If Satan casts out Satan, he is divided against himself." And He goes on to explain that to bind Satan requires one stronger than Satan. In verse 30 Jesus says, "He who is not with me is against me," and in verses 31 and 32 He explains that grieving the Holy Spirit is the unpardonable sin. Some would say that this is unconnected with the previous section, because our Bibles have a printed title "The Unpardonable Sin" above verse 31. However, note the connective. This section starts with the word "therefore." It is clearly a continuation of what Jesus has been saying in verses 22 to 30. So we must be very careful. We should be discerning, but we must be open and honest about our own ignorance and prejudices. If our security is in God, we need not feel threatened about learning things that we have previously been closed to. If, however, we have our security in being with other like-minded individuals who are closed to the gifts of the Spirit, then so be it. Of course we need to be discerning about copycat ministries; some do attempt things in their own strength, thinking that if they copy the manifestations they will experience the real thing. That is not the right way round, though.

Whatever the context, we must be very careful about attributing the work of God's Holy Spirit to Satan. The unpardonable sin is obviously a continual hardening of the heart toward God. It is the sin of total unbelief. However, unbelief has to start somewhere, and perhaps scoffing at the supernatural is just the thin edge of a wedge that we should have nothing to do with.

The Purpose of Signs and Wonders

Have you ever seen one of those movies where the good guy and the bad guy are battling it out in a casino over the roulette wheel or a game of poker? Have you noticed how the camera films very little of what is going on on the table? Instead, it is almost totally preoccupied with capturing every facial expression of the two opponents: every twitch of the lips, every threatening glare, every drop of sweat on the forehead. The stakes are raised, and the tension increases. Everyone knows that what's really at stake is not the small fortune that has been laid on the table, but the reputations of the players. The winner of this game, we all know, is going to be the ultimate winner of the larger battle that the film is all about. This is exactly what is going on when God works through a display of miracles—what is really happening is that God is taking on Satan in the heavenlies. To those caught up in worshiping idols or the occult, God is overthrowing their false gods with a supernatural display of power.

This principle was clearly demonstrated when Moses went into Egypt to rescue the children of Israel.

> Then the Lord spoke to Moses and Aaron, saying, "When Pharaoh speaks to you, saying, 'Show a miracle for yourselves,' then you shall say to Aaron, 'Take your rod and cast it before Pharaoh, and let it become a serpent.'"
>
> So Moses and Aaron went in to Pharaoh, and they did so, just as the Lord commanded. And Aaron cast down his rod before Pharaoh and before his servants, and it became a serpent.

> But Pharaoh also called the wise men and the sorcerers; so the magicians of Egypt, they also did in like manner with their enchantments.
>
> For every man threw down his rod, and they became serpents. But Aaron's rod swallowed up their rods. (Exodus 7:8–12)

Yes, Satan can work miracles, but, as Jesus said, there is one stronger than Satan, to bind him. Here God has demonstrated His superiority over the false idols worshiped by the Egyptians. The ultimate purpose of this demonstration of power was of course evangelistic: "'. . . and I will gain honor over Pharaoh and over all his army, that the Egyptians may know that I am the Lord.' And they did so" (Exodus 14:4).

A New Testament example occurs when some itinerant Jewish exorcists thought that they could imitate Paul and cast out demons, but the evil spirit said, "Jesus I know and Paul I know; but who are you?" and then the demon-possessed man beat them up. We are told that this resulted in the name of the Lord Jesus being magnified, and "many of those who had practiced magic brought their books together and burned them in the sight of all" (Acts 19:11–20).

One experience I had of God working supernaturally in this way was in Kuala Lumpur, Malaysia. My wife and I were there to visit a nearby refugee camp. As we walked around the city, we saw many invalids dotted about the sidewalk begging for money. Some were covered in scabs and sores and had very severe physical deformities; others looked as if they were in need of psychiatric treatment.

I remember feeling helpless and overwhelmed and thinking, "I wish I could give them more than just a few coins." Of course, I knew how Jesus had healed people like this, and so had some of the disciples. Yet that was then, and this was now. What could I do, if anything? I remember praying, "Lord, if you want to touch one of these dear souls in a supernatural way, help me to know, and give me the faith. Lord, I can't go around to everyone, but you can lead me to someone if you want to. I am willing."

Hilary and I then stepped inside a shop to buy film for our camera. As we did so, a tall man, who I can only describe as demon-possessed, came running into the shop screaming at us. It was a frightening sight: his eyes were rolling about in their sockets, and he was frothing at the mouth. He was covered with sores from head to foot, and he seemed to have had his sleeves and trouser legs rolled up expressly to expose them. Of course he wanted some money, but I knew beyond any doubt that God had answered my prayer, and wanted to do something in this man's life. The shopkeeper was furious and threw the fellow out. We followed him out into the street. The man's yells and grunts made no sense to us, and we knew that we couldn't just go through an evangelistic formula with him. So we laid hands on him, there and then in the street.

A large crowd had gathered by this time, and we started to pray in the Spirit for him. This was a new experience for us, and I don't know who was the more astonished, him or us. There we were, with one hand on him and the other in the air, praying out loud before a crowd of about thirty or forty people. It was a strange sight!

Then it happened. The man suddenly changed before our eyes from being a crazy, demon-possessed madman to a calm, serene, ordinary individual. A smile and astonishing peace came over his face. We put our arms around each other and hugged each other. He rolled down his sleeves and trouser legs, and all three of us walked calmly away. We put the man in touch with a church and gave him some literature. As we were moving on the next day, we couldn't have done much more, but I do know beyond any doubt that the Lord touched his life that day, and taught us something in the process.

God has made signs and wonders available to help us reach those who are deeply entrenched in the enemy camp. I receive many prayer letters from missionaries working in difficult situations throughout the world. I have noticed that many of these missionaries are beginning to say the same thing: that they believe the only way forward is to demonstrate the power of God to the people they are seeking to reach. This, of course, is not a substitute for preaching the Word, but a supplement (signs following); nor is it a substitute for living out the Christian life before them, the life of love and humility. The following chart may help us to understand more clearly.

Kingdom of Satan			Kingdom of God
Apathy	False gods and ideologies	Occult, witchcraft and Satan worship	Salvation

Apathy

To reach the apathetic, in some ways, is not easy. However, the apathetic are not as deeply entrenched in Satan's kingdom as others (although they are just as eternally lost). They do not believe in God or in anything supernatural. If they can be reached, it will probably suffice to present them with the gospel, while at the same time being very much in prayer for them.

False gods and ideologies

Now it gets a little more difficult! We are moving deeper into enemy territory: the realm of Eastern religions, cults, and extreme political groups. Usually the minds of these people are very closed, and their eyes are supernaturally blinded (as are those in the first group, but in this group even more so). It may be enough to reach them with the gospel message, but it would certainly be beneficial to have signs following, too.

Occult, witchcraft and Satan worship

Even further into the enemy camp. Much more is involved than a simple sharing of faith. Jesus warned that some evil spirits would only come out by prayer and fasting (Matthew 17:21). This is spiritual warfare at its greatest intensity. While God can still work through the gospel message, which is a powerful two-edged sword, He may well work through signs and wonders, too. Satan needs to be bound. The lost need to see that there is one who is more powerful. This is a very appropriate situation for the working of miracles, alongside the preaching of the Word.

Resurrection: The Ultimate Miracle

Personally, I am of the belief that the greatest miracle of all is when the vilest sinner repents and receives Jesus Christ as his Lord and Savior. This passing from spiritual death to life is what makes the angels in heaven sing. To see God reach down into the gutter of the world and pick up a fallen sinner and make something out of his life will always be to me the ultimate sign and wonder. However if, in a very rare case, it is going to take somebody actually being physically raised from the dead to achieve this, then so be it. I am open to it.

Why do we not hear about miracles like this today? Let me put forward two suggestions:

1. Resurrection was never meant to happen on a large scale because we are told, "It is appointed for men to die once" (Hebrews 9:27). We would not have been told this if Christians were meant to be going out en masse to empty all the graveyards.
2. In order for it to happen in unique cases and to bring glory to God, God would need to use a man or woman of the utmost humility and integrity. If power corrupts, and absolute power corrupts absolutely, it would be a rare individual who could have a ministry like this and not let it go to his head. However, it is not totally impossible. Let's look at how the apostle Paul dealt with it.

It was the day before Paul was due to leave Troas (Acts 20:7–12), and he had got a bit carried away with his preaching. The time was midnight, and young Eutychus had fallen asleep sitting in the window. As they were three floors up and the window was open, this wasn't a clever thing to do. Sure enough he fell out, and the fall killed him. Paul just matter-of-factly stopped the meeting for a few minutes, while he popped downstairs and brought Eutychus back to life. "Do not trouble yourselves," he said, "for his life is in him" (v. 10). He simply returned upstairs and continued with the meeting. In the morning Paul moved on to Miletus.

Just imagine if that were you or me. Would we have responded like that? This could be our ticket to fame and fortune: television appearances, book royalties, a cult following. This was not the way of Paul, which is why God could use him.

What was Peter's approach when he raised Tabitha from the dead at Joppa (Acts 9:36–43)? Notice that Tabitha is called a disciple, and that she was full of good works and charitable deeds. The body of Tabitha, who had died from an illness, rested in an upper room surrounded by weeping friends and relatives. What did Peter say? "Just you people watch me"? "Have no fear, Peter is here"? No, we are told that Peter put them all out of the room, and he kneeled down and prayed. How does this compare with our approach today? Peter showed great humility and dependence on God, but at the same time he knew that he could exercise authority in Jesus' name. He merely said, "Tabitha, arise," and she came back to life.

These two examples perhaps give us some insight as to why we don't see much of this kind of miracle today. God wants us to exercise faith; but can we be trusted with that much faith? When Paul healed a cripple at Lystra (Acts 14:10), the people wanted to make him and his partner, Barnabas, into gods. That has always been a temptation for man, hasn't it—to be like a god. Even back in the garden of Eden, Satan knew this particular weakness of ours. He said to Eve, "For God knows that in the day you eat of it [the fruit], your eyes will be opened, and you will be like God..." (Genesis 3:5).

So how did Paul and Barnabas deal with this temptation? The people of Lystra were now bringing oxen to sacrifice to their new "gods." We read:

> But when the apostles Barnabas and Paul heard this, they tore their clothes and ran in among the multitude, crying out and saying, "Men, why are you doing these things? We also are men with the same nature as you, and preach to you that you should turn from these useless things, to the living God..." (Acts 14:14–15)

Would that be our response? Would we try and get a book and film deal right away, and work the late-night chat show circuit, or would we be distressed that *we* were now the objects of the crowd's worship? Would we cry out and tear our clothes in anguish? This is how we must be if God is going to entrust us with dynamic, powerful ministries.

So can we expect God to work like this today, and use a believer to raise someone from the dead? As long as we understand that it would be the rare exception and not the rule, I believe the answer is yes. Instead of constantly trying to rob God's Word of its power because of our unbelief, we should humble ourselves before our great and awesome God, that we too might become the kind of people He can use to work miracles through.

God in a Box

Perhaps you've heard it said that we shouldn't try to put God in a box. By this we mean that we shouldn't seek to be the ones who determine how God can work. Don't we realize that, even if we wanted to, we couldn't? It is foolish to even think it.

Two thousand years ago they tried to put God in a box once and for all. The tomb where they laid Jesus being their equivalent of our six foot by two foot coffin! They found then, as we will find now, that when you put God in a box, in no time at all—it's empty!

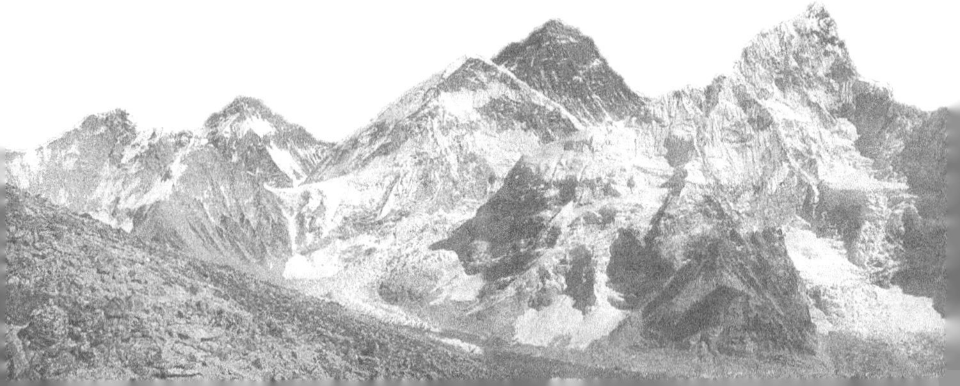

Chapter 11
FAITH IN THE DARK

Others were tortured, not accepting deliverance, that they might obtain a better resurrection. Still others had trials of mockings and scourgings, yes, and of chains and imprisonment.

They were stoned, they were sawn in two, were tempted, were slain with the sword. They wandered about in sheepskins and goatskins, being destitute, afflicted, tormented—of whom the world was not worthy. They wandered in deserts and mountains, in dens and caves of the earth.

And all these, having obtained a good testimony through faith, did not receive the promise, God having provided something better for us, that they should not be made perfect apart from us.

Hebrews 11:35b–40

When Things Go Wrong

George and Libby Senter went out to Liberia in 1980. For six years they did a good job, working with the Southern Baptist Foreign Missions. Then one day Libby caught a Liberian friend of the family molesting their ten-year-old daughter, Rachel. The man turned on Libby and stabbed her to death. He then turned on Rachel and killed her too. George was two hundred miles away picking up their son when the killings took place.[1]

Let's face it, things do sometimes go wrong, terribly wrong. It's hard to understand when suffering and tragedy come to those who have given up everything to follow Christ. It's hard to understand suffering, period. Perhaps we were never meant to. Of course death has no sting as far as the believer is concerned, but when it happens suddenly and brutally, as it did for the Senters in Liberia, then it would be wrong to dismiss it with a few pious platitudes. This is a serious issue. It deserves serious treatment as a mark of respect for all those who have lost their lives or suffered for the gospel's sake; who, as our text above, from Hebrews 11, implies, did not receive the promise in this life, but went on to something even better.

So far, we have looked at great exploits, miracles, amazing answers to prayer, and conquests of faith. These indeed should be the hallmarks of every believer who is hungry for God and determined to press on to get to know Him better. However, a diet of nothing but instant miracles is not good spiritual food. Real, true grit faith often has to be born in the dark, for darkness gives faith its opportunity to glow.

When the "Props" are Taken Away

What do we really put our trust in? In the affluent West, it is very apparent to anyone who has traveled that there is something lacking in the life of the average Christian. We see some Christians with their huge houses, brand-new cars, large bank accounts, insurance policies and all the rest of it, merrily traveling night after night to "faith" meetings. Here they will gladly use every opportunity to pray for the sick to be healed. They'll lay hands on anyone and everyone, and then return home to their warm beds, totally indifferent to the billions of people in the world who don't know Christ. Many of course do care about the lost, and it is not wrong to have a nice house if God has blessed you that way, but it can be hard not to become soft and indifferent if we live like that and are not careful.

I believe in healing, but such a faith as this, a faith which costs us nothing, is a mockery to God and to the thousands of pioneer missionaries who have given up everything to follow Christ. When faith starts to affect our own personal circumstances, our own living conditions, our own bank accounts, then it is a real faith, and our trust is in God alone and not in these things.

Now if we really mean business with God, we can expect that He is going to mean business with us. God may well have a vigorous discipleship program lined up for those who show potential. He's not going to waste His time on those who are unwilling to pay the price. That's not wise economy. But those who have said, "Yes, Lord, whatever it costs," those He will disciple and use. A. W. Tozer said that "God tells the man who cares."

Part of our training, though, will almost certainly involve some period of time when all the props to faith will be removed. This, however, can be a most liberating time, because we discover then that God really can be trusted.

A small boy was walking with his father by a river watching some workers who were knocking some temporary props out from under a bridge. "Look, Dad!" he said. "Why are they doing that? Won't the bridge fall down?" "No," replied his father, "it will just settle down on those big stone pillars. They will give it the permanent support it needs."[2] This is how it is with us when God removes all our human sources of security. We settle down on Him. He is our permanent support, and all that we need.

A letter from a missionary out in the jungles of New Guinea has captured the spirit of the faith that comes into its own when all props have been taken down:

Men, it is great to be in the thick of the fight, to draw the old devil's heaviest guns, to have him at you with depression and discouragement, slander, disease. He doesn't waste time on a lukewarm bunch. He hits good and hard when a fellow is hitting him. You can always measure the weight of your blow by the one you get back. When you're on your back with fever and at your last ounce of strength, when some of your converts backslide, when you learn that your most promising inquirers are only fooling, when your mail gets held up, and some don't bother to answer your letters, is that the time to put on mourning? No sir. That's the time to pull out the stops and shout Hallelujah! The old fellow's getting it in the neck and hitting back. Heaven is leaning over the battlements and watching. "Will he stick it?" And as they see who is with us, as they see the unlimited reserves, the boundless resources, as they see the impossibility of failure, how disgusted and sad they must be when we run away. Glory to God! We're not going to run away. We're going to stand![3]

When Opposition and Persecution Come

When God calls someone to a particular task, He will start testing him early on. Will he stick with it when he's misunderstood and criticized; when his friends turn against him; his financial resources disappear; his home disappears; the church rejects him; his family rejects him; he hears malicious gossip about himself being spread around? Some of these things, at least, will be the inevitable consequences of making our lives count for Christ.

The apostle Paul said, "For a great and effective door has opened to me, and there are many adversaries" (1 Corinthians 16:9). We should expect opposition, but it is hard when it comes from those from whom we would expect to receive support and encouragement.

I have tried to do much to help the Vietnamese refugees who have come to Britain. However, one situation I couldn't help them with occurred when some well-meaning English people wanted to obtain a building for them to use as a Buddhist temple. The world says that we should respect everyone's beliefs. But does that really make sense? Yes, we should respect people—with that I agree—and we should respect their right to believe what they want. But we don't have to respect those *beliefs*. No, not at all; especially when they are based upon fear and superstition, and can be very harmful.

As some of the people involved in this project were churchgoers, I felt that I should write and share my views. The moment I put the letter in the mailbox, a dark, oppressive cloud of depression settled down over me. For several days I couldn't pray or worship God; then I forced myself to. I realized that I had trodden on Satan's toes, and he didn't like it. So I made myself worship. I'm glad I did, because it was only the joy of the Lord that gave me strength to get through the next weeks. I received all kinds of nasty calls and hate mail. My letter was duplicated and passed out among the Vietnamese community and sent to national newspapers. One reporter was particularly aggressive. I was reported to the Race Relations Board as a Vietnamese- and Buddhist-hater. (At that time we had opened our home to nine Vietnamese Buddhists who had nowhere to live.) It was a difficult time. Some church leaders accused me of "damaging church relationships with secular agencies." God, however, led me to some well-known Christian leaders who, thankfully, gave me their full support. My view was that if the Vietnamese themselves organized a Buddhist temple, that was their business, but that it wasn't the job of those who profess to be Christians to encourage them in their darkness.

It must have surprised those who were causing the trouble, when they discovered that the Vietnamese community had a high regard for our work, and consequently were not interested in opposing us.

Jesus said, "Blessed are you when they revile and persecute you, and say all kinds of evil against you falsely for My sake. Rejoice and be exceedingly glad, for great is your reward in heaven, for so they persecuted the prophets who were before you" (Matthew 5:11–12).

My experiences could hardly be called persecution compared to those who really have suffered for Christ.

In Richard Wurmbrand's book *Tortured for Christ*, he gives us the following account of how God strengthens and gives courage to those who suffer for Him.

It was strictly forbidden to preach to other prisoners. It was understood that whoever was caught doing this received a severe beating. A number of us decided to pay the price for the privilege of preaching.

The following scene happened more times than I can remember: A brother was preaching to the other prisoners when the guards suddenly burst in, surprising him halfway through a phrase. They hauled him to the "beating room." After what seemed an endless beating, they brought him back and threw him, bloody and bruised, on the prison floor. Slowly, he picked his battered body up, painfully straightened his clothing and said, "Now brethren, where did I leave off when I was interrupted?"[4]

On the outside this brother was bloody and messy, but on the inside he had joy and peace. The same could not be said of the wardens—inwardly they must have been going through their own private hell as they witnessed such courage.

Testimonies like this show how foolish the accusations of some nonbelievers are, that "Christianity is a crutch for the weak." What nonsense! The history of the Church is a history of unparalleled heroism. It is a history of thousands who have suffered, been tortured and died for Christ. Let anyone who doubts it read *Fox's Book of Martyrs*, if they have the stomach to get through it. And persecution is not just a thing of the past—many today are still suffering and laying down their lives for their Savior. Christians are the most courageous people in the world. Don't let anyone tell you otherwise!

When the Thorn Just Won't Come Out

C. T. Studd had been a wealthy man, but he gave all his money and riches away to follow Jesus. He went out to China to work with

Hudson Taylor. Because of his relentless labors and sacrificial living there, he became seriously ill. He was so sick that the doctors called him "a museum of tropical diseases."

In fact, C. T. Studd came back to England a broken man. One day he was walking in town and saw an announcement for a missionary rally. The notice said, "Cannibals Need Missionaries." He laughed at the implications of that wording, but still he went to the rally. There God called him to be a missionary to Africa.

He was already a grandfather and still a desperately sick man, but he went to the heart of Africa where no missionary had ever been. He worked day and night to give the native people the gospel. During those seventeen pain-racked years, he did not go home on furlough once, and in those years he saw his wife, Priscilla, only one time. He loved her, his children and his grandchildren, but he wanted them to be in Britain to organize the home front—the prayer force.

Because of the pain he was experiencing near the end of his life, C. T. Studd was often given painkilling drugs to help him continue. His personal attendant, Jimmy Taylor, a Baptist, was there with him. One night he thought that Studd was definitely dying, so he went over at eleven o'clock to give him a couple of shots to kill the pain and knock him out so that the great missionary could sleep.

At about 3 A.M. Taylor became concerned and thought he had better go and check to see if Studd was still alive. When he arrived at the hut where Studd lived, he was shocked to find it empty. On the table was a little note. It read, "Dear Jim, I have translated a couple more chapters of Acts, and I am off now on my bicycle to reach another tribe for Jesus. They have never heard of Him."[5]

If you want to pause for a moment and let the full impact of that sink in, I fully understand.

Whenever I think of C. T. Studd, I picture in my mind an old, sick man pedaling from village to village with the gospel, because "They have never heard of Him." And we can't even make it to the prayer meeting because we have a cold!

I don't for one moment believe that sickness finds its origin with God. The Book of Job shows us clearly that sickness originates with

Satan, not with God. God, though, can permit Satan to inflict us, and it would seem that, in His sovereign wisdom, He sometimes decides not to take the "thorn in the flesh" away, but to use it for His glory in other ways.

I'm a great believer in praying for the sick to be healed. I have done it myself many times. Also, others have prayed for me, and I have been miraculously healed. I believe that God is in the business of healing the sick, whether it be through medical means or by direct supernatural intervention. In James 5:14–15a we read: "Is anyone among you sick? Let him call for the elders of the church, and let them pray over him, anointing him with oil in the name of the Lord. And the prayer of faith will save the sick, and the Lord will raise him up." The Bible could not be any clearer than that. The prayer of faith will save the sick.

Now at this point I confess that this is something I do not fully understand. Are we to believe that C. T. Studd never prayed a prayer of faith concerning his illness? Throughout history there have been many great men and women of faith who have not been delivered from such illnesses. The only explanation I can offer is that our faith must be born out of love for God; for who He is, not for what He does for us. This was the message of the Book of Job. This is Hebrews 11 type faith, a faith that does not need to understand everything, because it trusts the One who is in control.

We know that God can and does heal. We know that He can and does deliver from danger, but the power of our testimony is this: that even if He doesn't, it makes no difference. "And this is the victory that has overcome the world—our faith" (1 John 5:4).

And God's power is made perfect in weakness. Paul had to suffer with his "thorn in the flesh" so that he would understand that God's grace was all that he needed (2 Corinthians 1:7–10).

Would we have been as challenged and moved by C. T. Studd's testimony if he had been a fit, young athlete instead of a sick, old grandad? Know that it is when we are weak that we are strong (2 Corinthians 12:10).

If you are in a position where that "thorn in the flesh" just doesn't seem to want to come out, then I would ask you to consider something. Can you see things as God sees them? Minnesota is known as the state that has ten thousand lakes. However, if you fly over Minnesota it looks more like a sea with ten thousand islands; there is water everywhere. From God's view, things look different. Perhaps you've heard the story of the little hamster who tried and tried to escape from his cage. All he could see were the metal bars that kept him a prisoner, and he was so frustrated by it all. What he couldn't see, however, was that outside the cage there was a huge, fierce dog just waiting to pounce on him if he got out. Don't let circumstances get you down; trust in your heavenly Father, for He alone sees the big picture. You may have a "thorn in the flesh," but trust that He knows best; His Grace is all that you need.

When Failure and Discouragement Come

Have you set out to do the Lord's work, and failed? Just when you thought all was well, Satan tripped you up. Charles Swindoll has often taken comfort from these words by Theodore Roosevelt:

> It is not the critic who counts: not the man who points out how the strong man stumbled or where the doer of deeds could have done them better. The credit belongs to the man who is actually in the arena; whose face is marred by dust and sweat and blood; who strives valiantly; who errs, and comes short again and again, because there is no effort without error and shortcoming; who does actually try to do the deed; who knows the great enthusiasm, the great devotion and spends himself in a worthy cause; who at the worst, if he fails, at least fails while daring greatly.
>
> Far better it is to dare mighty things, to win glorious triumphs even though checkered by failure, than to rank with those poor spirits who neither enjoy nor

suffer much because they live in the gray twilight that knows neither victory or defeat.[6]

During the Second World War, the allies had their fair share of casualties. They certainly didn't win every battle, but they did win the war! As believers in a spiritual war that we know is already won, we should not even consider giving up because we've taken a few casualties along the way.

Satan just loves to exploit situations like this and discourage us with his lies. A classic example is found in Zechariah 3:1–10. Satan accuses Joshua, the High Priest, but what does God say? "The Lord rebuke you, Satan! . . . Is this not a brand plucked from the fire?" Know your rights as a believer, and don't let Satan drag you down.

I don't care who you are, if you're on the front line, constantly attempting the impossible for God, you will have your setbacks and times of discouragement. Be realistic about this; every cloud has its silver lining. Your breakthrough may be just around the corner. Charles Haddon Spurgeon used to say:

> Before any great achievement, some measure of depression is very usual . . . This depression comes over me whenever the Lord is preparing a larger blessing for my ministry.[7]

Once I had to speak at short notice to a group of street sleepers in Chicago. Whenever I have to speak to people in that type of situation, I make sure that I can spend time with them first. They do not need preaching at, but loving into the kingdom. I asked the Lord to help me know what I should say. He whispered to my heart, "Tell them that they are not 'down and outs' in My sight. They may be down, but with Me they are certainly not out." You may feel down, but know this—with God you're certainly not out, and never will be.

Another time I was speaking in the maximum-security prison, Belmarsh, in southeast London. I started by telling the prisoners that in God's eyes, they deserved to be in there. I quickly followed this up by saying that in his eyes, though, they were no worse than anyone else. No worse even than the prison officers standing around guarding them. I told them, "You have broken the law, so you are in here. but God says that we 'have all sinned and fallen short of the Glory of God.' If the pass mark for the exam is 50 percent, it doesn't matter if you got 49 percent or 10 percent—you have failed." God hasn't finished with you, He is the Once Again God, the God of the second chance. He sent Jesus to die for you and me. So don't make excuses: admit and confess your sin. The cross doesn't do excuses; it does repentance.

When Death Comes

When Anglican vicar and evangelist David Watson found out that he had terminal cancer, he was reminded of these words written by Dostoevsky: "It is not as a child that I believe and confess Jesus Christ. My 'hosanna' is born in the furnace of doubt."[8]

David Watson was a man of God. His life and ministry had a tremendous impact on me. He was greatly loved, and is now greatly missed. Yet his ministry lives on. Like Abel, he still speaks today (Hebrews 11:4).

Keith Green was another man with a dynamic ministry who died young, in a plane crash that took both him and two of his children suddenly. He left behind a bewildered widow, Melody, who was expecting their fourth child. Yet the ministry of Keith Green lives on.

There is no escaping it; it comes to us all sooner or later. One day we have to die. However, when it comes sooner and there are family members left behind, it is so very hard to understand. And perhaps this is our greatest test of faith.

When I was nineteen years old, I was in a horrific car crash. Traveling at 85mph, our car went out of control, overturned, and continued rolling over for a quarter of a mile, before finally coming to a halt, upside-down. There were two of us in the front; my friend who was driving, and myself. He was killed outright and had the most terrible injuries to his body. I was completely untouched. I walked away without a scratch.

I don't fully understand it, and often feel guilty that I survived, as did my two friends in the back. This experience certainly made us more aware of the fragility of life. There are many times in my life which I can look back on and see how the hand of God has protected me. Once, in Argentina, I was nearly shot! However, none of us knows how long we have. So what does death mean?

> But I do not want you to be ignorant, brethren, concerning those who have fallen asleep, lest you sorrow as others who have no hope. For if we believe that Jesus died and rose again, even so God will bring with Him those who sleep in Jesus . . . And the dead in Christ will rise first.
> (1 Thessalonians 4:13–16)

In more recent years we seem to have moved away from presenting a gospel to the unsaved that talks about heaven and hell and life after death. This is a great pity, even a tragedy. Look again at the passage from Thessalonians and notice these few poignant words: "as others who have no hope."

I remember going to the funeral of a non-Christian friend. At least, as far as I know he wasn't a believer. I felt as though I was the only one singing the hymns at the church. The atmosphere was one of sorrow and grief, which you would expect at any funeral, but it was also one of hopelessness and despair. It had a great impact on my life, and made me even more committed to getting the gospel message out.

In comparison, a Christian funeral is very different. There is sadness at the loss, yes. There is grief and sorrow, true; but there is also hope and, yes, even joy. That is what happens when Jesus comes to live in your heart. Our tears of sadness can also be tears of joy, even at the graveside of a loved one, because Jesus is risen—and so shall we be. Hallelujah!

And so this is the message of Hebrews chapter 11, perhaps summed up well for us in these words of Paul in his letter to the Romans:

> Who shall separate us from the love of Christ? Shall tribulation, or distress, or persecution, or famine, or nakedness, or peril, or sword? ... For I am persuaded that neither death nor life, nor angels nor principalities nor powers, nor things present nor things to come, nor height nor depth, nor any other created thing, shall be able to separate us from the love of God which is in Christ Jesus our Lord. (Romans 8:35, 38–39)

This is the most powerful testimony that any of us can have. It is this confidence that should spur us into action to serve our Lord, to do great exploits.

When Shadrach, Meshach and Abed-Nego were thrown into the fiery furnace, they gave this testimony to the king: "Our God whom we serve is able to deliver us from the burning fiery furnace ... But if not ..." (Daniel 3:17, 18). This was no lack of faith on their part, rather it was the greatest expression of faith that we can ever have. We need to stop seeing God as a benefactor, and instead love Him for who He is. Our lives will take on a whole new dimension when we go to spend eternity with him. As the apostle Paul said, "And why do we stand in jeopardy every hour?" (1 Corinthians 15:30)

Daniel knew his God. It made him strong, and he carried out great exploits. What about you and me? Will we spend our lives playing Trivial Pursuit?

> And God said to Daniel, "But you, go your way till the end; for you shall rest, and will arise to your inheritance at the end of the days" (Daniel 12:13).

Amen. Even so, come, Lord Jesus!

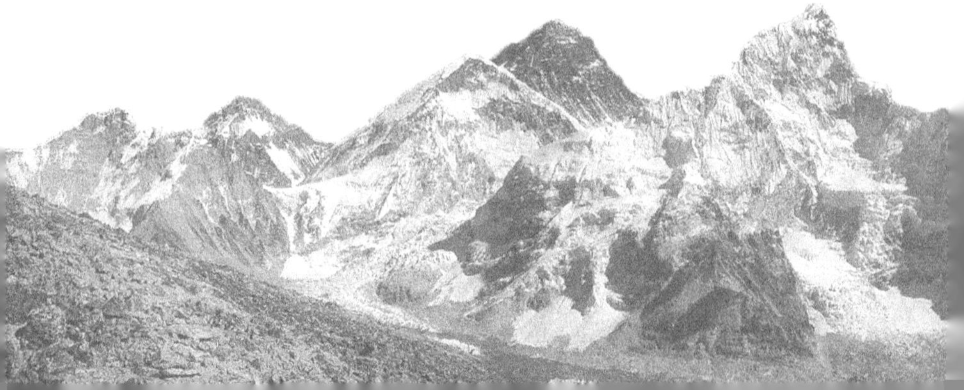

Chapter 12
THE CHALLENGE OF THE IMPOSSIBLE

Therefore we also, since we are surrounded by so great a cloud of witnesses, let us lay aside every weight, and the sin which so easily ensnares us, and let us run with endurance the race that is set before us, looking unto Jesus, the author and finisher of our faith, who for the joy that was set before Him endured the cross, despising the shame, and has sat down at the right hand of the throne of God.

Hebrews 12:1–2

THE LOOK IN THAT WOMAN'S FACE STILL HAUNTS me today. I was in a refugee camp in Malaysia, and she had just pleaded with me to help her find her missing thirteen-year-old daughter. "When did you last see her?" I naively enquired. "In boat, in boat, on sea, China Sea, pirates come—they take," was the reply. The awful truth took some time to penetrate. Their frail refugee boat had been attacked by pirates on the South China Sea, and several young girls had been taken away. This was nothing new to me at the time. I had already been on a ship that had rescued some of these boat people, and I knew all about the atrocities firsthand.

However, I had never been asked, challenged even, to do something about it. I felt helpless.

Unknowingly, this lady and her husband had touched a sensitive spot with me. I had already started a mission in England to help the boat people, but I was inwardly wrestling with the issue of what to do about this problem in the South China Sea. After all, I was out in Asia to tell these people that God loved them and had a wonderful plan for their lives! I was also telling them how great and mighty our God is and that nothing is too difficult for Him. Could I really bring that message, and ignore their plea for help at the same time?

I told the family that my wife, Hilary, and I would do everything we could to find their girl, but that they were not to expect too much. Was I lacking in faith? Perhaps, but I didn't want to build their hopes up, for I knew what it meant when pirates kidnapped young girls; it began with rape and ended with them either being sold into prostitution or murdered. We searched all the refugee camps in Singapore, Malaysia, and Thailand. Most we visited ourselves; the others we checked through the United Nations. We never did find her.

The parents went to live in America, and I had to write to them and tell them the awful truth. They were obviously heartbroken, but thankfully they turned toward God and not away from Him. They now attend a Baptist church in California.

It was in Songkhla that I made up my mind. It was on the beach at Songkhla, where many bodies, some eaten away, of Vietnamese men, women and children had been washed up, that I kneeled down and prayed. Through tears I cried out to God. I can't remember what I said, but I do know that it went something like this: "Oh God, I've given up everything to follow You. About all I have left are my Bible and my Second Mate Navigation Certificate. Lord, I can navigate a ship, and I trust completely in Your promises. Am I to believe that nothing can be done for this situation? Lord, I don't believe it. Give me the faith I need to trust You. Lord, please give us a ship."

It seemed like a crazy prayer at the time. After all, the "us" was not much more than Hilary and myself. We had no money, no backing, no crew, and yet I couldn't accept that God did not want to do something about this, and was not looking for someone to stand in the gap. No, I could not accept that the word "impossible" was meant to be a part of our vocabulary as believers. As Hudson Taylor said, "There are three phases of Christian work—impossible, difficult, done!"[1]

I have a friend who is a Native American, and who has a great desire to spread the gospel among the Native American community. It is not uncommon to find him prostrate, crying out to God for his people, and believe me, the Native American peoples of North America are a people in great need. Look at the facts:

There are 573 Native American tribes, speaking 169 languages.

The income level of Native Americans is 69 percent – 31 percent less – of what other Americans make.

American Indian/Alaska Natives have twice the infant mortality rate of non-Hispanic whites.

American Indian/Alaska Native infants are twice as likely as non-Hispanic white infants to die from sudden infant death syndrome (SIDS).

American Indian/Alaska Native infants are 2.7 times more likely than non-Hispanic white infants to die from accidental death before the age of one year.

The US suicide rate is up 33 percent since 1999, but for Native American women and men, the increase is even greater: 139 percent and 71 percent, respectively, according to an analysis published in November 2019 from the Centers for Disease Control and Prevention's National Center for Health Statistics (https://www.cdc.gov/mmwr/volumes/67/wr/mm6708a1.htm).

Suicide disproportionately affects non-Hispanic American Indian and Alaska Natives, according to the CDC. A March 2018 CDC report found that their suicide rate was more than 3.5 times higher than those among racial and ethnic groups with the lowest rates.

Suicide rates vary by race and ethnicity. In 2017, the age-adjusted rate of suicide among American Indians/Alaska Natives was 22.15 per 100,000, and among non-Hispanic whites it was 17.83.

In contrast, the suicide rate among Asian/Pacific Islanders was 6.75, the rate for blacks was 6.85, and the rate among Hispanics was 6.89.

Among American Indians and Alaska Natives, suicide rates peak during adolescence and young adulthood, then decline. This is a different pattern than is seen in the general United States population, where suicide rates peak mid-life.[2]

I asked my friend, Darrell, what was holding his ministry back, for he was clearly frustrated. "We don't have the tools to do the job," he said; meaning, I think, that there wasn't much support for the work. "And many Christians," he continued, "don't believe God can do anything. They think it's impossible!" He uttered the word "impossible" with a mixture of sadness and disgust. He wasn't being judgmental but simply venting his frustration in his desire to see them reached.

Is there such a thing as an impossible situation, to God? As God once said to Abraham, "Is anything too hard for the Lord?" (Genesis 18:14) No, no, a thousand times no; we must never allow ourselves to believe it. Our God is the God of the impossible. He delights to do the impossible, especially if He can do it through ordinary people. We are ordinary people, and He is our great God. As it has been said:

> It is not great faith we need:
> but faith in a great God!

Now, I hear you say, "That's all well and good, but what has it to do with me, a filing clerk in Wisconsin (or Yorkshire, England)?" It has everything to do with you, for we are talking primarily about principles, not projects. Francis Schaeffer said, "With God there are no little people, there are no little places."[3] You are the salt in your community, and it's a community that needs shaking. The question is: are you living a totally surrendered life? Do you believe that God can use you?

And what about the wider world? Are we in prayer for the two billion Muslims who are without Christ? Or do we not even care? What about the one billion Hindus, the 1.3 billion Han Chinese, the hundreds of millions of Buddhists? Have you ever said to God, "I'm willing to go, if that's what you want"? Are you supporting those you know who have gone? Would you be willing to burn your boats? Brother Andrew, founder of Open Doors, an organisation that supports persecuted Christians worldwide, doesn't believe that there are any closed countries. He says, "I can tell you how to get in, but I may not be able to tell you how to get out again."[4]

Keith Green's song "Asleep In The Light" contains some of the most powerful and challenging words I've ever heard in a song. I doubt that anyone could hear him sing them and not be affected. Here they are:

> Do you see, do you see
> All the people sinking down?
> Don't you care, don't you care
> Are you gonna let them drown?
> How can you be so numb
> Not to care if they come?
> You close your eyes
> And pretend the job's done.
> "Oh bless me Lord, bless me Lord,"
> You know it's all I ever hear.
> No one aches, no one hurts,
> No one even sheds one tear.
> But He cries, He weeps, He bleeds
> And He cares for your needs
> And you just lay back
> And keep soaking it in.
> Oh can't you see it's such sin?
> 'Cause He brings people to your door
> And you turn them away
> As you smile and say,
> "God bless you, be at peace."
> And all heaven just weeps,
> 'Cause Jesus came to your door.
> You've left Him out on the streets.

> Open up, open up,
> And give yourself away.
> You see the need, you hear the cries,
> So how can you delay?
> God's calling, and you're the one,
> But like Jonah you run.
> He's told you to speak
> But you keep holding it in.
> Oh can't you see, it's such sin?
> The world is sleeping in the dark
> That the church just can't fight
> 'Cause it's asleep in the light.
> How can you be so dead
> When you've been so well fed?
> Jesus rose from the grave
> And you, you can't even get out of bed.
> Oh, Jesus rose from the dead,
> Come on, get out of your bed.
> How can you be so numb
> Not to care if they come?
> You close your eyes
> And pretend the job's done.
> You close your eyes
> And pretend the job's done.
> Don't close your eyes
> Don't pretend the job's done.[5]

Perhaps we don't have any problem getting out of bed, but maybe we can't drag ourselves away from the television, internet, or from looking at the brochures for next year's holiday. These are difficult times we live in. They are times when we need to stand up and be counted; to resist the satanic onslaught on our society; to be like Martin Luther, whose testimony was, "Here I stand, I can do no other."[6] It's a time to tackle the impossible, but only those who know their God will be strong and carry out great exploits. Do you know your God? If not, the responsibility to get to know Him lies with you alone. Remember, "He is a rewarder of those who diligently seek Him" (Hebrews 11:6b).

Run With God

God does not leave us "in the air," as it were, after Hebrews 11, thinking, "That's great, but what do I do now?" The first two verses of Hebrews chapter 12 are part of the message, too. (Note the connecting word, "therefore," that begins Hebrews 12:1.)

What is God saying to us in these two verses? A paraphrase would read something like this:

> Come on now, what more do we need to see to be convinced? Look around at the people God has raised up to lead us. Look at the heroes of the faith in the Bible. We can do it, too!
>
> Only, let's throw off all our doubts and worries and negative thinking. Resolve to get right with God, and to walk before Him in holiness. Then we shall run the race of faith set before us. All we need to do is to keep looking to Jesus. He is the author and finisher of our faith. He is the one who's already run the race. He endured the cross and despised the shame, for the joy set before Him, and now sits at the right hand of the Father.

Yes, Jesus has run the race, and He calls us to follow Him. Will we run with Jesus, or will we run with the world?

> I saw the runner far away in the distance, moving rapidly against the horizon. His run was neither furious nor agonized. Yet he seemed to have a goal, for his movement was resolute, vigorous, and confident.

Watching him as he ran, I was touched by the effort he made. I was also somewhat ill at ease within myself. The running figure inexplicably seemed to make a demand upon me. I felt intuitively that he wanted me to run with him, try to match his pace, and share in some measure both the demand and the fulfillment of the race.

However, I succumbed to insecurity and fear. Shielding my eyes, I turned away and moved slightly in the opposite direction.

Now I knew that I was also a runner.

I ran alone.[7]

There are only two directions to run, either toward God or away from Him.

Get Up and Grow

I shall always remember those five messages on Jonah that Dr. Alan Redpath gave at Spring Harvest[8] some years ago. At one point, he talked about when he was a young man training to be a rugby player. His workout sounded grueling: pull-ups, push-ups, sit-ups; you name it, and he was doing it. He even used to push hard against the walls of his apartment with his shoulders, toughening them up so that he would be better in the scrum. The point was, of course, to show the lengths that people are prepared to go to, to train for something like that. How much more should we be in training for the Lord? How much do we discipline our lives, study God's Word, and pray? Are we willing to invest a couple of years of our life at Bible college, or with short-term discipleship missions, such as Operation Mobilization and Youth With A Mission?

I met Alan Redpath once, at a conference for evangelists in Swanwick, Derbyshire, England. I was eager to find out what he was doing. "He must be retired, of course," I thought to myself. "After all, he's way past retirement age. He must live in some home for retired missionaries in the countryside, I suppose." I was in for a shock! He was living with his wife in a high-rise apartment block in Birmingham, in the West Midlands of England. They were one of the few white families in the building. His heart was broken because everywhere he looked from his window he saw mosques. Allah dominates the Birmingham skyline.

When Billy Graham came to Birmingham for one of his Mission England meetings, he knew that he could count on Dr. Redpath's support. But what role did this great man of God play? Where did the former pastor of Moody Memorial Church, Chicago, see his role? It shook me to the core when I found out. Alan Redpath, an old man suffering with his health, had been going with his wife door-to-door, to tell people about Jesus and invite them to the meetings. He had several doors shut in his face and was even reported to the authorities.

Come on now! What's *our* excuse? Now that we are surrounded by so great a cloud of witnesses, and the God of the impossible has made his dwelling place with us, let us move out in faith to achieve the impossible. Let's put the milk away and start eating solid food. This is no time for Trivial Pursuit—it's time for Great Exploits. Let's get up and grow!

If Hebrews 11 and the first two verses of Hebrews 12 are not enough, let's look at the last verse of Hebrews 10.

> But we are not of those who draw back to perdition,
> but of those who believe to the saving of the soul.
> (Hebrews 10:39)

Oh, great and mighty God, nothing is too difficult for You. Great and wonderful God, the one who lives in my heart.
Here am I.
Come—shake the world.

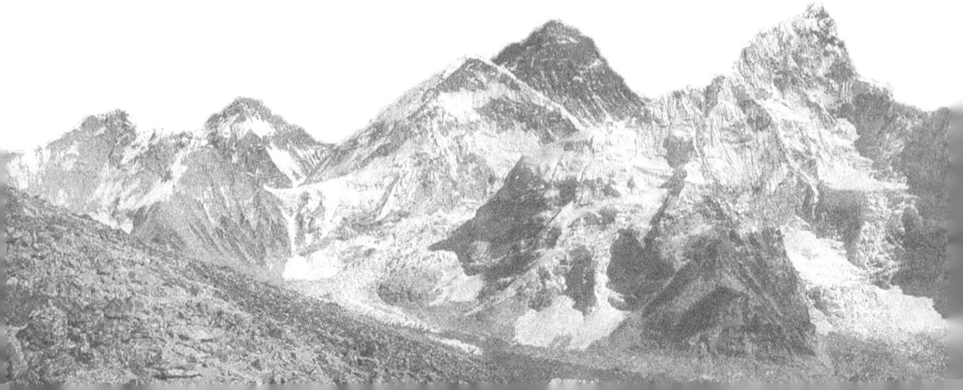

Postscript

ONE YEAR AFTER WRITING THE FIRST EDITION of this book, Maurice, his wife Hilary, and a group of young people, bought a ship in Holland. After three months doing her up and renaming her "The Redeemer," they embarked on nine years of ministry, living by faith and seeing amazing answers to prayer, as God used them and many others from around the world to reach into many countries and situations. With a foreword by Roger Forster and an endorsement from Jackie Pullinger, you can read this incredible testimony to God's faithfulness in Maurice's book *Close to the Wind*, also published by Xulon and available from Amazon, Barnes & Noble, many bookshops, from Seacare in London (CCP Trust, PO box 24224, London SE12 0ZW, vitsea1@aol.com) and from Ichthus Christian Fellowship's online bookshop. It is also available directly from Xulon in Florida.

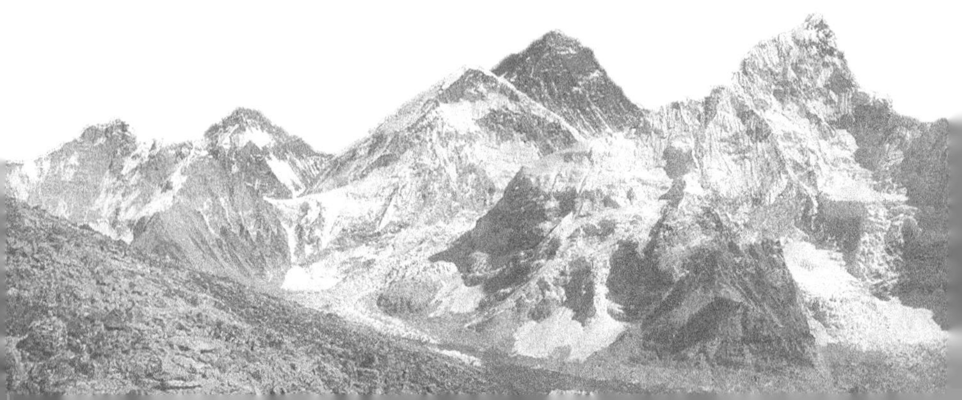

Notes

Chapter 1: The Dynamics of Faith
1. From a message given by Jackie Pullinger at a church in Paris, France and from private correspondence.
2. Taken from *Rees Howells Intercessor* by Norman Grubb (Fort Washington, Pennsylvania: Christian Literature Crusade, 1952), pp. 129–133.
3. 'heathen' could also read 'unbelievers.' John Geddie, as noted in J. Oswald Sanders, *Spiritual Leadership*, Chicago, IL: Moody Press, 1967, n. 24.
4. Taken from *Is That Really You, God?* by Loren Cunningham and Janice Rogers, Grand Rapids, Michigan: Chosen Books, Zondervan, 1984, p. 30.
5. Taken from *Billy Graham* by John Pollock, Grand Rapids, Michigan: Zondervan, 1966, p. 17.
6. From the hymn "My Hope Is Built On Nothing Less," words by Edward Mote, 1834.
7. Colonel Jack Lousma, "Nine and a Half Weeks in Space," *Voice Magazine,* Vol. 33, No. 7, Costa Mesa, California: FGBMFI. July 1985, p. 2.
8. Arvella Schuller, *The Positive Family,* New York: The Berkley Publishing Group, 1982, p. 30.
9. Gordon MacDonald, *Ordering Your Private World,* Nashville, Tennessee: Oliver Nelson, 1984, p. 130.

Chapter 2: Faith At the Dawn of History
1. Hudson Taylor, *Hudson Taylor's Spiritual Pilgrimage,* Melbourne, Australia: Austral Printing and Publishing Co., Ltd, p. 48.
2. William Temple, *Readings in St. John's Gospel,* London: Macmillan and Co. Ltd, 1963, p. 24.
3. Andrew Murray, as quoted in *Leadership* magazine, Carol Stream, IL: Christianity Today, Inc., Fall 1985, p. 129.
4. Dr. David Yonggi Cho, *The Fourth Dimension,* Plainfield, New Jersey: Logos International, 1979, p. 95.

Chapter 3: Go With God
1. Jackie Pullinger, *Chasing the Dragon,* London: Hodder and Stoughton; Servant Publishers in the USA.

Chapter 4: Battleship to Glory, or Caribbean Cruise?
1. W. Burgess McCreary, *John Bunyan: The Immortal Dreamer,* Anderson, Indiana: Warner Press, 1928, n. 3.
2. Samuel Stevenson, *"Where is God's Power?" Poems That Preach,* compiled by John R. Rice, Wheaton, Illinois: Sword of the Lord Publishers, 1952, n. 78. Used by permission.
3. Catherine Marshall, *Beyond Our Selves,* New York: McGraw-Hill Book Co. Ltd., 1961, p. 162.
4. Taken from *William Carey, Cobbler to Missionary* by Basil Miller. Copyright 1952, 1980 by the Zondervan Publishing House. Used by permission.

Chapter 5: No Turning Back
1. Louis Fischer, *Gandhi, His Life and Message for the World,* New York: Mentor Books, 1960, p. 34.
2. Corrie Ten Boom, *In My Father's House,* Old Tappan, New Jersey: Fleming H. Revell Co., 1976, dustcover.

Chapter 7: You Call This A Christian Family?

Notes

1. "Two Children." Written by Steve and Annie Chapman © copyright 1986 by Dawn Treader Music. All rights reserved. Used by permission of Gaither Copyright Management.
2. "Something Beautiful." Words by Gloria Gaither. Music by William J. Gaither. © Copyright 1971 by William J. Gaither. All rights reserved. Used by permission.

Chapter 8: The Faith of the Leader
1. Information about Operation Mobilization can be obtained from: OM, Quinta, Weston Rhyn, Oswestry, Shropshire, SY10 7LT, England.
2. Taken from *Billy Graham* by John Pollock, Grand Rapids, Michigan: Zondervan, 1966, p. 94.
3. Hudson Taylor, *Hudson Taylor's Spiritual Pilgrimage*, Melbourne, Australia: Austral Printing and Publishing Co., Ltd., p. 48

Chapter 9: Where the Action Is
1. Rabbie Burns, as taken from *Explore the Book*, Vol. 3, by J. Sidlow Baxter. Grand Rapids, Michigan: Zondervan, 1960, p. 237.
2. Some of these insights were gained from a message given by Ray Mayhew at Ichthus Christian Fellowship in southeast London in 1986.

Chapter 10: Raising the Dead
1. R. R. Cunville, "The Evangelisation of Northeast India," an unpublished D.Miss thesis for Fuller Seminary's School of World Missions, 1975, D. 156–179. As quoted in John Wimber, *Power Evangelism,* Sevenoaks, Kent, England: Hodder and Stoughton, 1985, p. 173.

Chapter 11: Faith In the Dark
1. "Baptist Missionary Murdered in Liberia," *Moody Monthly,* February 1987, p. 42. Used by permission.

2. Henry G. Bosch, *Our Daily Bread,* Grand Rapids, Michigan: Radio Bible Class, 1986, reading for February 13, 1987. Used by permission.
3. "Letter From a Missionary in New Guinea," Dallas Theological Seminary Book of Illustrations.
4. Richard Wurmbrand, *Tortured For Christ,* Glendale, California: Diane Books, 1969, p. 43.
5. Brother Andrew, *Building in a Broken World,* Wheaton, Illinois: Tyndale House Publishers, 1981, pp. 46–47. Used by permission of the author.
6. Theodore Roosevelt, speech before the Hamilton Club, Chicago, April 10, 1899, as cited in Charles Swindoll *Hand Me Another Brick,* Nashville, Tennessee: Thomas Nelson, 1978, p. 79.
7. J. Oswald Sanders, *Spiritual Leadership,* Chicago, Illinois: Moody Press, 2007 edition, pp. 160–161.
8. David Watson, *Fear No Evil,* Wheaton, Illinois: Harold Shaw Publishers, 1984, p. 43. (First published in Sevenoaks, Kent, England by Hodder and Stoughton.)

Chapter 12: The Challenge of the Impossible
1. Hudson Taylor, as quoted in J. Oswald Sanders, *Spiritual Leadership,* Chicago, Illinois: Moody Press, 1967, p. 123.
2. Bill Haas and Paul Straubel, Center for Indian Ministries, Oak Hills Fellowship, Bemidji, Minnesota. Used by permission.
3. Francis A. Schaeffer, *No Little People,* Downers Grove, Illinois: Inter-Varsity Press, 1974, dustcover. (Published in England as *Ash Heap Lives,* Norfolk Press, 1975.)
4. Brother Andrew, *Building in a Broken World,* Wheaton, Illinois: Tyndale House, 1981, p. 19.
5. "Asleep In The Light" by Keith Green © 1978 Birdwing Music/Cherry Lane Music Publishing Co., Inc./Ears To Hear Music. All Rights Reserved. Used courtesy of the Sparrow Corporation, 9255 Deering Ave., Chatsworth, CA 91311 USA. International Copyright Secured.

NOTES

6. Roland H. Bainton, *Here I Stand,* Nashville, Tennessee: Abingdon Press, 1950, p. 144.
7. Malcolm Boyd, *The Runner,* Waco, Texas: Word Books, 1974, p. 7.
8. Spring Harvest is a Christian festival/conference held in Britain every year and is sponsored jointly by *Christianity* magazine and British Youth for Christ.

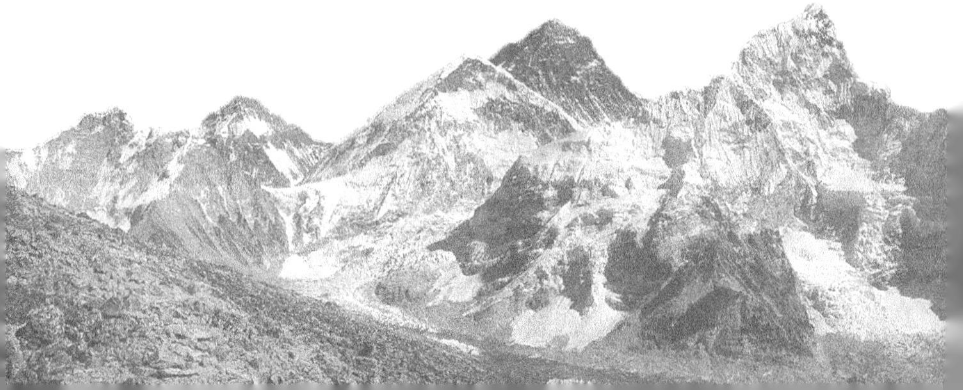

Also by this Author

'This is a gripping, faith-raising true adventure story'

Roger Forster
Founder of Ichthus Christian Fellowship

CLOSE to the WIND
The Story of a Youth Group that Bought a Ship

'It brings a wistfulness for the adventures that God has for every one of us'

Jackie Pullinger

Foreword by Roger Forster

MAURICE VITTY

Available from Amazon (paperback or Kindle)

For further info: CCP Trust, PO Box 24224, London SE12 0ZW
vitsea1@aol.com

Lightning Source UK Ltd.
Milton Keynes UK
UKHW010150071220
374731UK00001B/26